CONTENTED COWS

Give Better Milk

THE PLAIN TRUTH ABOUT EMPLOYEE RELATIONS
AND YOUR BOTTOM LINE

By

Bill Catlette

&

Richard Hadden

Saltillo Press
Germantown, Tennessee

Permissions Department
Saltillo Press
7608 Poplar Pike
Germantown, TN 38138
(901) 756–4661
E-Mail: WillifordS@aol.com

Publisher: Steve Williford
Editor-in-Chief: Robbin Brent
Associate Editor: Trent Booker
Cover Design: Patterson Graham Design Group
Interior Design: Electronic Publishing Services, Inc., Tennessee

Library of Congress Cataloging-in-Publication Data

Catlette, Bill and Hadden, Richard.
    Contented Cows Give Better Milk: the plain truth about employee relations and your bottom line / Bill Catlette and Richard Hadden.
        p.   cm.
ISBN 1-890651-04-4
1. Business.   I. Title.

Printed on approved acid-free paper
10 9 8 7 6 5 4

Dedication

To Mary and Christine

CONTENTS

FOREWORD

Few would disagree that treating people right, whatever right means, is generally good business practice. After all, it is one of the few truly timeless principles of life itself. But in the world of business, as in life, how many organizations and leaders actually manage to operationalize that premise consistently—day in and day out, rain or shine? Is it because we're unable to grasp the concept? Hardly. The concept is simple as dirt. Do we lack the authority (individually), or maybe the funds (institutionally) to make it happen? Nope. Neither has anything to do with it.

Rather, despite our (and we do mean our) best intentions, we seem to get derailed by a blizzard of fads on the one hand, and near-term urgencies cross-dressed as strategic imperatives on the other. While we have yet to see anyone proclaiming that treating people badly is somehow good for business, we have yet to see a compelling, unemotional case made for the converse. In a similar vein, business bookshelves and boardrooms are cluttered with the all too predictable (and easy) prescriptions for empowerment, teaming, restructuring, and the like.

So this book is an effort to establish a bottom-line-based case for the principle that if you treat people right, you'll make more money, period. It represents a challenge to each of us. Because once a clear and compelling reason to do something is established, and the path is made just a little brighter, it all comes down to a personal decision. You either act or you don't.

Throughout the book, we have used a somewhat conversational tone … a little too conversational to suit our editor. But we've hung with it for a reason, actually two of them. First, neither of us especially enjoys being lectured to or preached at and we suspect you feel the same way. Second, it is about to become abundantly clear that in each of our cases, our first avocation is not as a writer, but as a business person for whom the lessons and advice contained on these pages are as relevant as for any reader.

Titling a book is not easy. That was particularly true in this case. We were told that the book's essence must be conveyed in six or fewer words, and the clearer and more memorable, the better. To us, the use of the cow as a metaphor seemed highly appropriate. To understand the metaphor as we intend it, one should focus not on any unflattering physical characteristics which may be attributed to members of the bovine species, but on the fact that for hundreds, perhaps thousands of years, cows have served as productive life partners and indeed as measures of wealth and stature. For those who might be put off by a comparison of working people to cows, get over it.

Though we felt strongly about it, we struggled with the *contented* part, on two fronts. Our first concern was that some might confuse the term *contented* with adjectives like happy, carefree, giddy, kinder-gentler, etc. If you need to, look it up. That's not what it means ... anything but. It represents *exactly* what we mean to convey: *A person's degree of satisfaction with their work situation is entirely and directly related to their output.*

The second problem had to do with the expression *Contented Cows* which, it turns out, is a trademarked expression, the rights to which are owned by Nestle. No fewer than four attorney friends (How's that for an oxymoron.) told us in no uncertain terms, "Don't even think about it." So we went ahead and asked anyhow. We are eternally grateful to the folks at Nestle for their understanding, support, and having the good heart to say "yes."

With the rationale and the path clear, let's proceed.

ACKNOWLEDGMENTS

This book was an ongoing project for better than two years. In the course of researching, writing, and publishing it, we relied on the efforts of many. We are, and will continue to be, grateful for their assistance. Here are just a few of the people without whose help we couldn't have done it. ...

Our publisher and partner, Steve Williford, whose gracious good humor is as beneficial as his literary and publishing skills.

Our editor-in-chief, Robbin Brent, who pushed, cajoled, worked tirelessly, and neither offered nor accepted any excuses. Associate editor, Trent Booker, who wordsmithed, gracefully put up with our foibles, and voluntarily learned more about cows than any non-dairy farmer should have to.

Pat Patterson, who designed the most outrageous cover we've seen on a business book, and Rick Soldin, who took a pile of stuff and made it look like a real book.

Brad Ziemba, who spent several days in the University of Memphis library checking and re-checking the numbers, and Karey Bakker, who interviewed many of the sources within the companies we've featured.

Wayne Morris, Jane Lemmon, Beth Irvine, and Tom Ladet, who spent countless hours reading the manuscript for us, and who cared enough to tell us the truth.

Corporate chieftains Truett Cathy, David Graham, Dennis LeStrange, Sal Quadrino, Dennis Spina, and Mike Smith, who supported our effort with their ideas, their good example, and their time.

For sharing information about their respective companies, we thank Heather Jardim of Kingston Technologies, Betty Kahn of Crate & Barrel, Scott Mayson and Jerry Johnston of Chick-fil-A, David Russo of SAS Institute, and Valerie Wagner of Starbucks Coffee ... as well as so many others we've met informally in our travels, and who were kind enough to answer our questions.

We also thank fellow members of SHRM, who helped us define and refine the lists of *Contented* and *Common Cows*.

Tom Peters, who, without even knowing it, served as an inspiration.

Our friends and virtual company partners, Matt Starcevich and Steve Stowell, who have given so willingly of their time, ideas, and advice.

Jim and Loretta Weirauch and Chris Roessler, for their administrative, technical, and moral support.

The professional writers and journalists at business publications like *Fortune, Business Week, INC*, and the *Wall Street Journal*, whose work has fueled our passion.

The folks at Nestle. Without their support, this book would have a very different title.

And, to our families, who have been there through every single minute of this journey, we say "thank you."

INTRODUCTION

How Do The Best Get Better?

Indeed, the chief reason for our failure in world-class competition is our failure to tap our work force's potential.[1]

—Tom Peters

What is it that permits one organization to achieve unprecedented levels of success over a substantial period of time, while a nearly identical competitor is struggling or going down the tube? Is success the result of better mousetraps, dumb luck, or maybe just better execution? Consider, for example:

• How could Southwest Airlines achieve 23 consecutive years of record revenues and sustained profitability while TWA, Continental, Pan Am, Eastern, Braniff and others all around them were hemorrhaging red ink and going broke for the first (and maybe even second) time?

• How can GE, at a plant near Columbia, Tennessee, produce refrigerator compressors at a cost which is 20 percent less than that of its foreign competitors, despite an unfavorable labor cost differential of $15 per hour?

• In an industry long given up for dead with its heavily unionized workforces and draconian work rules—how can the Union Pacific and Burlington Northern/Santa Fe Railroads be undergoing a remarkable resurgence, with dramatically improving levels of customer service and profitability?

• Finally, will somebody please explain how, in an industry long dominated by foreign (notably Pacific Rim) competitors, Ohio-based Worthington Steel can produce steel with a quality level far in excess of the industry average, and, relative to sales, is able to outearn its Pac Rim competitors by a wide margin?

In each of the aforementioned cases, and in every other success story we have been able to find, there are some strikingly similar approaches being taken. Our mission is to discover, chronicle, and help others replicate some of those approaches. As Thomas Edison said, "There is a better way. ... Find it!"

FATTENING THE CALVES

For approximately 30 years following the end of World War II, American companies and their workers enjoyed something of a "bubble of prosperity." Relatively unscathed compared to Europe and Japan, we were the lone industrial powerhouse left standing in the world. As a result, nations around the globe became captive markets for American goods and services (not that they weren't already clamoring for them). We enjoyed a fat and happy existence, counting the riches that came from having a monopoly on the supply side of the trade equation. Millions entered the workforce, dutifully accepted raises every six months, watched their health care and other "bennies" get better and cheaper, and the workweek get shorter. Amidst what Federal Reserve Board Chairman Alan Greenspan would have termed "irrational exuberance," millions of people allowed themselves to believe that our newfound affluence was a God-given right. *Risk* was a vanishing four-letter word, and, with the rest of the world seemingly down for the count, things like quality and productivity were deemed irrelevant.

POOF! The bubble burst as America awakened from its collective dream to discover that not only was the race not over, but we were on pace to finish well back in the pack. As managers across the land desperately began to reassert themselves, the blaming, rationalizing, and over-reliance on silver-bullet solutions commenced. Much was written and said at the time about the demise of commercial enterprise in the United States, that:

- we were being outdistanced by foreign competitors who took advantage of an uneven playing field,
- greed and corruption had created dangerous and destructive economic forces,

- the "New Age" workforce couldn't read, and wouldn't work,
- the blame for our economic woes rested squarely on the shoulders of a misguided, ineffectual government,
- we couldn't compete because our culture was out of tune with the modern marketplace,
- maybe we just lacked the will to succeed.

Depending on one's perspective, all or none of this may have seemed true. True or not, all that really mattered was that, in many markets and in many respects, we *were* being outperformed by others. No ifs, ands, or buts about it. All anyone had to do to find evidence (if further proof was really needed) was look at our national trade deficit; or note the change in market share of foreign vs. domestically produced products for just about any item imaginable; or compare rates of productivity growth and standard of living in the U.S. with any of a host of countries; or just listen for Ross Perot's "giant sucking sound." It wasn't and, in some cases, still isn't a pretty sight.

Obviously, though, a lot has occurred over the intervening period as many businesses in the U.S. have undergone radical and revolutionary change. Change, sometimes painful, gut-wrenching change, accompanied by more than a little confusion. Businesses by the hundreds have merged and de-merged, restructured and re-engineered, downsized and rightsized, teamed and empowered, outsourced and co-sourced. Frenetic though this activity was (and still is), it has resulted in good, substantive changes being made to the way American companies do business.

But should we mourn the death of the "good ole days?" Days when the pressure wasn't as great as it is today? When jobs were secure? When paychecks were fattened at regular intervals with scarcely any regard for worth or performance? When employees did what they were told out of fear, and the "Big Mother" corporation did everyone's worrying for them? For those who might say "yes," we've got a little advice:

GET A GRIP! Stop and think for a moment, and you'll realize that the good-ole days really weren't so terrific after all. Was it fun having someone else do all your thinking for you? Or, did you really enjoy having to think and take responsibility for other adult human beings? Remember what it felt like to do a job that was too narrowly defined to begin with, and then get micro-managed on top of it? How about being constantly second-guessed by legions of staff specialists in the cheap seats? How comfortable were you knowing that no matter how good a job you did, your performance and pay were going to be looked at pretty much the same way as that of everyone else? Did you like having one or two drones—co-workers (we wouldn't think of calling them peers) whose last productive act occurred too long ago to even be remembered—taking up space (and precious oxygen) in your workgroup? We didn't think so.

BUZZWORDS ARE THE PROBLEM, NOT THE SOLUTION

Over the last two decades, there has been no shortage of quick-fix, silver-bullet solutions and how-to scenarios. We suspect that much of any benefit wrought by "vogue-word" management theories has come as the result of their forcing companies to inadvertently trip over some ugly truths about the neglected state things were in—realizations we likely would not have come to any other way.

Yet, despite the billions we've spent launching one well-intentioned managerial fad (for example, PIP, QWL, Participative Management, Teaming, Empowerment, etc.) after another, not much has changed about human nature since Elton Mayo's first studies of the relationship between motivation and productivity at the Hawthorne Works of the Western Electric Company in the late '20s. That was nearly 80 years ago! Before anyone but his mother had ever *heard* of quality guru/curmudgeon Dr. W. Edwards Deming; before the word Toyota had ever been uttered in the Western Hemisphere; and before Tom Peters, author of mega-bestselling management classics like *In Search of Excellence* and *Thriving on Chaos,* was even born!

DISCRETIONARY EFFORT - SPEEDBRAKE OR AFTERBURNER

In a series of motivational experiments entitled the Harvard Studies, Mayo, using a real company, real managers, and real employees, first uncovered the unmistakable relationship between worker attitudes and production, or output. Essentially, Mayo learned two things:

1. That human beings are uniquely capable of regulating their involvement in and commitment to a given task or endeavor.
2. That the extent to which we do or do not fully contribute is governed more by *attitude* than by necessity, fear, or economic influence.

In a nutshell, what he learned (and what has been reinforced by a number of subsequent experiments) is that there is an increment of human effort which can be applied exclusively at the discretion of the individual. This finding led to the coining of the term "Discretionary Effort" (DE), which is defined as the difference between that level of effort which is minimally necessary, and that of which we are in fact capable. It represents the difference between obedience and high performance, and between those who are *managed* versus those who are *led*. Its expenditure is completely a matter of choice.

PERSONAL CAPABILITY

− MINIMUM REQUIREMENTS

= DISCRETIONARY EFFORT

The context within which Mayo discovered DE at Western Electric was one in which employees were, for a variety of reasons, withholding it. They were performing only at a minimally satisfactory level or, as some might put it, they kept coming to work (and getting paid) even though, for all intents and purposes, they were on strike.

The only difference between then and now is that back then, because of a fairly jobless economy and the absence of protective empowerment (the result of union-sponsored legislation), the withholding of discretionary effort was practiced in a much more covert manner. However, shortly after the conclusion of Mayo's studies, organized labor emerged as an economic force, and their weapon of choice was collective bargaining power. Its commercial implications confirmed Mayo's discovery and brought discretionary effort "out of the closet."

IT'S YOUR PEOPLE, STUPID

As Richard Pascale of the Stanford Graduate School of Business put it, "The trouble is, 99 percent of managerial attention today is devoted to the techniques that squeeze more out of the existing paradigm—and it's killing us. Tools, techniques, and how-to recipes won't do the job without a higher order ... concept of management."[2]

As managers career wildly from one tactic (e.g., customer satisfaction) to another (e.g., re-engineering), many forget that the critical difference between a brilliant strategy and one that gets successfully executed resides in the hearts and minds of people ... your workforce. We can scream, exhort, and rattle the saber all we want, but successful organizational change cannot come about without willing participation.

In many cases, putting alternative precepts into *practice* flies dead in the face of a definition of the managerial role that's been held and nurtured for literally hundreds of years, namely the old, authoritarian, plantation-mentality scenario which features the manager as order giver, and the employee as order taker. This failure to change our outlook toward the management of human effort has, for many, become the chief impediment to competitiveness, here and elsewhere. We certainly don't lack the brains, ability, or technology.

Rather, it's a matter of *will*; specifically, the will to change. Some have it, and some haven't gotten there yet.

Our purpose is to incent those in the latter category by calling attention to a few organizations that *do* "get it," and the very real, hard, bottom line impact they (and their shareholders) are enjoying as a result.

SUMMARY

1. Buzzwords are the problem, not the solution. Those organizations which have enjoyed the greatest and most lasting commercial success in our society owe that success not to vogue-word management theories, but to something else.

2. People make the difference, period. Each of us has direct and unilateral control over the amount of discretionary effort we choose to make available to the organization.

PERSONAL CAPABILITY

− MINIMUM REQUIREMENTS

= DISCRETIONARY EFFORT

3. Tools, techniques, and how-to recipes won't do the job without a higher order concept of management. Some things, like the good-ole days and plantation-mentality management, belong in our rear-view mirror.

SECTION ONE

THE PREMISE

JUST THE FACTS

Everyone is entitled to his own set of opinions, but no one is entitled to his own set of facts.

—James Schlesinger

THE XYZ 500: IT'S LIKE A BROKEN RECORD AT THE TOP OF THE CHARTS

Every year, respected business publications like *Fortune, INC,* and *Business Week* rank those companies that are doing the best job in their chosen industry or market. We read about the Most Admired and Best Managed, those generating the Highest Shareholder Return, Greatest Market Value, the XYZ 500; and the list goes on.

Caught in this annual downpour of rankings and ratings, we can't help but notice that with almost monotonous regularity the organizations nailing down these honors are the same ones, year after year. You know the names: Coca Cola, Merck, GE, Southwest Airlines, Intel, Nordstrom, 3M, USAA, Johnson & Johnson, and Hewlett-Packard, to list only a few.

Outside the corporate boardroom, but no less engaged in the world of business, lies the arena of professional sports. Here, too, the same teams perennially rise to the top—dynasties like the San Francisco 49ers, Los Angeles Dodgers, and Chicago Bulls.

Since 1982, *Fortune* has published an annual listing of the "Most Admired Corporations," ranking—overall and by industry—those organizations with the best business reputations. Approximately 11,000 corporate executives, outside directors, and financial analysts judge companies according to the following criteria:

- quality of management
- quality of products and services
- value as a long-term investment
- use of corporate assets
- financial soundness
- innovativeness
- community and environmental responsibility
- ability to attract, develop, and keep talented people

In the 1996 version of this report, *Fortune's* Anne B. Fisher noted a thread running through the list when she wrote that "12 of the top 15 have great brands."[1] Likewise, she would have been correct had she observed that *all* of those same top 15 companies also happen to be regarded as exceptional places to work. In fact, nine of them have at one time or another been included in the *100 Best Companies to Work for in America.*[2] Similarly, *none* of the "100 Best" companies shows up in (or anywhere near) the bottom 50 on *Fortune's* list.

COMPANY	MOST ADMIRED RANK	SCORE	"100 BEST"
COCA COLA	1	8.70	—
PROCTER & GAMBLE	2	8.55	YES
RUBBERMAID	3	8.35	—
JOHNSON & JOHNSON	4	8.32	YES
INTEL	5	8.30	YES
MERCK	6	8.26	YES
MICROSOFT	7 (TIE)	8.23	YES
MIRAGE RESORTS	7 (TIE)	8.23	—
HEWLETT-PACKARD	9 (TIE)	8.19	YES
MOTOROLA	9 (TIE)	8.19	YES
3M	11	8.08	YES
PFIZER	12	8.06	—
DISNEY	13 (TIE)	8.05	YES
MCDONALDS	13 (TIE)	8.05	—
GILLETTE	15	8.00	—

In similar fashion, and on the premise that organizations are best known by their competitors, *Fortune* asked executives to rate companies in their own industries on measures like quality of management, financial soundness, and innovation. Here again, the results could hardly be more compelling. In case after case, the best places to work showed up at or near the top of industry rankings.[3] Some examples:

INDUSTRY	COMPANY	RANK	"100 BEST"
COMPUTERS & OFFICE EQUIP.	HEWLETT-PACKARD	1	YES
AIRLINES	SOUTHWEST	1	YES
PACKAGE & FREIGHT DELIVERY	FEDEX	2	YES
ELECTRONICS	GE	3	YES
SCIENTIFIC, PHOTO, CONTROL EQUIPMENT	3M	1	YES
COMPUTER & DATA SERVICES	MICROSOFT	1	YES
PUBLISHING & PRINTING	R.R. DONNELLEY	2	YES
ENTERTAINMENT	DISNEY	1	YES
PHARMACEUTICALS	JOHNSON & JOHNSON	1	YES
PHARMACEUTICALS	MERCK	2	YES
CHEMICALS	DUPONT	1	YES
BUILDING MATERIALS	CORNING	1	YES
SOAPS & COSMETICS	PROCTER & GAMBLE	1	YES
GENERAL MERCHANDISE	WAL-MART	1	YES
GENERAL MERCHANDISE	NORDSTROM	2	YES
GENERAL MERCHANDISE	J. C. PENNEY	3	YES
APPAREL	LEVI STRAUSS	1	YES
FURNITURE	HERMAN MILLER	2	YES
METALS	NUCOR	2	YES

For those who require a little harder financial evidence, the same publication, in December 1996, published an article based on Stern Stewart & Company's ranking of 1,000 corporations. Utilizing what many consider to be the two most effective measures of financial performance, Stern Stewart rated the corporations by Market Value Added (MVA), and Economic Value Added (EVA).[4] As its name implies, MVA describes the extent to which a company's stock has, over its lifetime, either enriched or impoverished investors. It shows the difference between what they have put in and what they can take out. EVA, on the other hand, represents a company's after-tax net operating profit minus its cost of capital (both debt and equity).

In this case, eight of the top 10 companies rated on MVA also appear among the *100 Best Companies to Work for in America*. Five corporations (Coca Cola, Johnson & Johnson, Merck, Microsoft, and Procter & Gamble) made the top 10 on *both* the "Most Admired" and "Highest MVA" lists, and four of those five also happen to be "100 Best" companies.

COMPANY	MOST ADMIRED RANK (SCALE = 1–417)	MVA RANK (SCALE = 1–1,000)	"100 BEST"
COCA COLA	1	1	—
MERCK	6	3	YES
MICROSOFT	7	5	YES
JOHNSON & JOHNSON	4	6	YES
PROCTER & GAMBLE	2	8	YES

At the opposite end of the spectrum, some organizations with not so stellar reputations as employers wind up near the bottom of the "Most Admired" or MVA/EVA rankings, or both. In many respects they are neither winning organizations, nor are they perceived as especially great places to work.

COMPANY	MOST ADMIRED RANK (SCALE = 1–417)	MVA RANK (SCALE = 1–1,000)
KMART	415	996
GENERAL MOTORS	288	998
US AIRWAYS	414	538
TWA	417	—

WHERE'S THE BEEF?

So what's the point? Actually, it's a simple one. So simple, in fact, that Carnation Company may have put it best many years ago when they suggested that their condensed milk product came "From Contented Cows."[5]

Any dairy farmer will tell you that for as long as cows have been milked, methods of care have been employed to produce healthier, more contented, and, most importantly, higher-yielding cows. In a similar vein, those organizations that can be consistently identified as winners in their respective fields, whether it's making jet aircraft engines or pharmaceuticals, delivering urgent packages, writing auto insurance policies, or merely "playing games," also happen to be known as some of the best places on earth to work. Unlike the age-old conundrum of the chicken and the egg, in this case we don't think there is any doubt about which came first.

From the start, the exceptional organizations have differentiated themselves as employers of choice, thus enabling them to hire and retain top-drawer people, and *then* differentiated their products and services in the marketplace. Think it's a coincidence? We don't.

We have a lot to say about what *Contented Cow* companies are doing, but perhaps just as notable is what they *aren't* doing. Unlike the approach being taken by many of their competitors, the management of these companies is not betting the ranch that technology and capital spending alone will lead them to a more competitive posture. But don't confuse contentment with complacency. The fact that a cow is contented in no way interferes with its inclination or ability to "jump over the moon." Instead, companies that follow the *Contented Cow* path seem to be in agreement with the idea, beautifully expressed by Owen (Brad) Butler, former chairman and CEO of Procter & Gamble, that "productivity comes from people, not machines."

> *From the start, the truly excellent organizations have differentiated themselves as employers of choice.*

It has been said that "the only way for any organization to ensure its financial security is by creating satisfied, loyal customers."[6] To the extent that the organization is at all labor-dependent, we propose that the principal requirement for operationalizing that aim is the creation of a satisfied, fully engaged workforce. In the main, our products and services, technology, methods, tools, and strategies can *all* be copied. But it's not as easy to duplicate a focused, caring workforce. In the final analysis, "people factors" are frequently *the* key source of competitive

advantage—the factor least visible to the naked eye and most difficult to emulate. Sooner or later, we must come to grips with the
fact that most businesses aren't so much capital- or expertise- or
even product-driven as they are PEOPLE-driven.

That hasn't always been the case. Under the earliest business
model, the corporation was little more than a tangible piece of
property—at first a piece of real estate (for example, a farm), and
later a factory. Then over time it became the financiers, those who
had supplied the capital necessary to expand and automate the
farm or factory, who emerged as the primary centers of influence.
But as the very nature of work continues to evolve, and its focus
shifts more to knowledge, service, and speed, the significance of
the hard assets and those who technically own them diminishes.
From now on, corporations will be defined less by their tangible
presence and more by the real pulsating bodies who comprise
them—customers, employees, and owners.

*Take away my factories, and I will build a new and better factory; but
take away my people, and grass will grow on the factory floor.*
—Andrew Carnegie

JUST THE FACTS

To determine if there was any factual basis to our premise about
Contented Cows and better milk, we first set out to identify a
group of companies which are widely recognized as being
employers of choice. We weren't interested in identifying those
outfits that have somehow managed to garner a good reputation
quickly. Rather, we focused on the ones that have done it the hard
way—over at least a 10-year period—and have managed to keep
their reputations intact through good times and bad. Nobody ever
drowned in honest sweat.

We relied on three main sources to separate the *Contented
Cows* from the rest of the herd:

1. The book, *100 Best Companies to Work For in America* (1984, 1985 and 1993 editions). Four of the six *Contented Cow* companies made the '84 list, and five of them made it in '85 and again in '93, with Southwest finally included in the most recent version. (In our view, they should have been there sooner. It's one of the few late arrivals anybody has seen from Southwest.)
2. Our colleagues in the Society for Human Resource Management, who have been consulted extensively on the subject.
3. Our own judgment based on 20-plus years of business experience. In the final analysis, we asked ourselves this question: "Is this a company that we would be proud and pleased to work for?"

Our task was made more difficult by the fact that we felt it important to identify organizations that were fairly representative of the broad spectrum of commerce. We included some from heavy manufacturing, some from the service sector, some from the world of high tech, some from retail, etc. You get the picture. While we ultimately settled on six organizations as the *Contented Cow* representatives, a handful of others easily could have qualified, including some strong personal favorites like Johnson & Johnson, Disney, Citicorp, Marriott, and Intel.

After the *Contented Cows* were identified, our focus then shifted to the task of finding comparable organizations, or *Common Cows*, against which to benchmark them. We first identified organizations in the same basic business or industry. Then, we searched for companies that compete in a significant way with the the six *Contented Cows*, and that most people would recognize. Size was not an issue. Nor did we attempt to bias the research by culling and keeping acorn calves (mismatched weaklings), against which to run the exemplars. It would have been quite easy, for example, to pit the U.S. Postal Service against FedEx; or TWA, or the now defunct Eastern Airlines against Southwest. (It was hard to resist the temptation, but somehow we managed.)

Our purpose is not (repeat, NOT) to bash one set of companies or to hold the *Contented Cow* group out as models of perfection, because they aren't. It *is* an attempt to validate something that we feel has for too long existed only as a sentimental notion on the part of many. We hope to alter this misperception and illuminate, from a somewhat different perspective, some of the distinct and valuable advantages of effective employee relations practices.

We've identified the 12 *Contented Cow* and *Common Cow* companies for the aforementioned reasons. But we didn't limit our research to these comparison organizations. Throughout the following chapters, we'll give examples gleaned from both personal experiences and interviews with people from many other organizations, some of which will no doubt be familiar to you. However, in all of our analysis, the test for being considered a *Contented Cow* company required that the organization meet the following minimum criteria:

1. **Profitability** – a consistent track record of growth in revenue and earnings.
2. **Continuity** – in business for at least five years (except in industries younger than five years, as in the case of Netscape, and a few other high tech firms.)
3. **Desirability** – be generally regarded by the people who work there as good places to work, with positive, affirming, sensible, and affordable employee relations practices.

THE FINE PRINT

From the start, we readily admit that real (and lasting) success in business requires more than just enlightened employee relations practices. You must have market-worthy products or services, the ability to deliver them when and where the customer wants at a price they're willing to pay, and, to be sure, capable leadership.

We also recognize that just as productive employees are not always satisfied, satisfied employees are not always productive.

In fact, some may be satisfied because they don't *have* to be productive. And, of course, there are those who prefer to "check their brains" at the door and work only with their bodies (if at all). So, we are not asking you to accept the notion that the ONLY factor explaining the huge financial performance advantage of the *Contented Cow* companies happens to be their employment practices. But, we *are* asking you to consider the possibility that

> *Just as productive employees are not always satisfied, satisfied employees are not always productive.*

it's impossible for any labor-intensive business to get to (let alone stay at) the top *without* having adopted such practices. We think the facts and figures you're about to see make the case in no uncertain terms. You be the judge.

In the course of our research, we pored over 10 years' worth of financials for dozens of companies. For comparison purposes, we settled on the 10-year period from 1986 to 1995, and on financial measures that were statistically significant, universally available, and commonly understood. Having established the background and parameters, here is our list of comparison companies:

CONTENTED COWS	COMMON COWS
HEWLETT-PACKARD(HWP)	TEXAS INSTRUMENTS (TXN)
FEDEX (FDX)	CONSOLIDATED FREIGHTWAYS (CNF)
GENERAL ELECTRIC (GE)	GENERAL MOTORS (GM)
SOUTHWEST AIRLINES (LUV)	UNITED AIRLINES (UAL)
WAL-MART (WMT)	SEARS (S)
3M (MMM)	XEROX (XRX)

Has anyone ever sung the glory of the cow?[7]
—Frank Lloyd Wright

Now, before going any further, ask yourself this question: "Based on what I know of these companies, which of them would *I* go to work for?" In fact, while you're at it, why not make a list of your own comparison companies? That way, if you at all doubt our premise, you can check their financials and see for yourself. Go ahead, it's okay to write in the book—you paid for it.

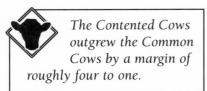

The Contented Cows outgrew the Common Cows by a margin of roughly four to one.

My list of Comparison Companies:

CONTENTED   **COMMON**

1. _____   _____

2. _____   _____

3. _____   _____

4. _____   _____

5. _____   _____

SIGNIFICANT OBSERVATIONS:

1. As shown in the following table, and again in Figure 1.1, at the beginning of the measurement period (1986), the *Common Cow* companies were, in aggregate, nearly three times the size of their *Contented Cow* counterparts, measured in annual revenues.

CONTENTED COWS	'86 REV. (MILL)	COMMON COWS	'86 REV. (MILL)
GE	36,782	GM	102,814
LUV	769	UAL	7,119
MMM	8,602	XRX	9,781
FDX	2,573	CNF	2,124
HWP	7,102	TXN	4,974
WMT	8,451	S	44,282
Total	64,279	Total	171,094
Avg.	10,713	Avg.	28,516

Source: Moody's

FIGURE 1.1

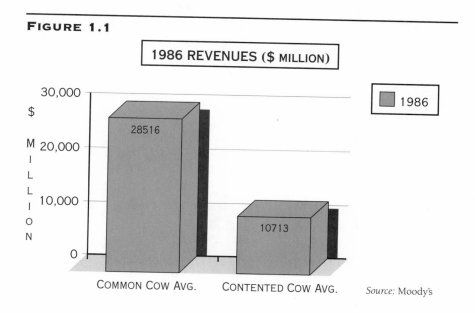

1986 REVENUES ($ MILLION)

Source: Moody's

2. Over the ensuing 10-year comparison period (1986–1995), the initial revenue gap was closed significantly as the *Contented Cows* outgrew the *Common Cows* by a margin of roughly four to one. (See Figure 1.2)

FIGURE 1.2

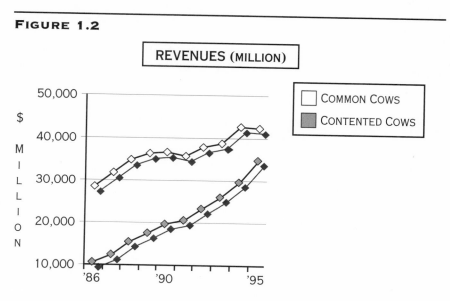

REVENUES (MILLION)

3. Performance in the sales growth area is not simply a matter of "averages beating averages." In *five out of six cases*, the *Contented Cows* outgrew the *Common Cows* by a substantial margin; the lone exception was Xerox, which nudged out 3M by a hair.

10 YEAR SALES GROWTH

COMPANY	% GROWTH	COMPANY	% GROWTH
GE	90.39%	GM	64.21%
LUV	273.60%	UAL	109.90%
MMM	56.48%	XRX	69.83%
FDX	265.02%	CNF	148.63%
HWP	343.80%	TXN	163.93%
WMT	876.14%	S	-21.13%
AVG.	317.57%	AVG.	89.23%
WEIGHTED AVG.	226.34%	WEIGHTED AVG.	48.29%

Source: Moody's

4. On the premise that companies in the same line of business should be somewhat comparable in their degree of labor dependence and the skill mix required of their workers, AND that, all things being equal, they would enjoy relatively the same levels of employee productivity, we examined both revenue and income figures on a per-employee basis.

As shown in figure 1.3, the 10-year sales growth comparison is every bit as stark when cast in this fashion.

Figure 1.3

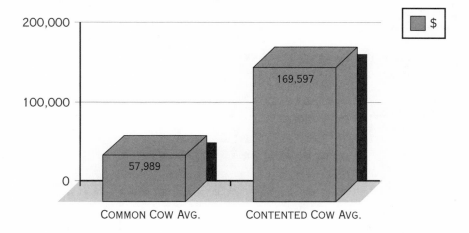

10 Year Revenue Growth/Employee (Mean)

$

200,000

100,000

0

169,597

57,989

Common Cow Avg. Contented Cow Avg.

Contented people give better performances.[8]

—Tommy Lasorda

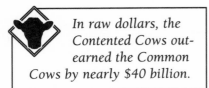

In raw dollars, the Contented Cows out-earned the Common Cows by nearly $40 billion.

5. Performance of the *Contented Cows* relative to their *Common* counterparts on the profit front is equally as compelling, if not more so. As shown in Figure 1.4, net income of the *Contented Cows* grew by 202 percent over the 10-year period, versus 139 percent for the *Common Cows*.

FIGURE 1.4

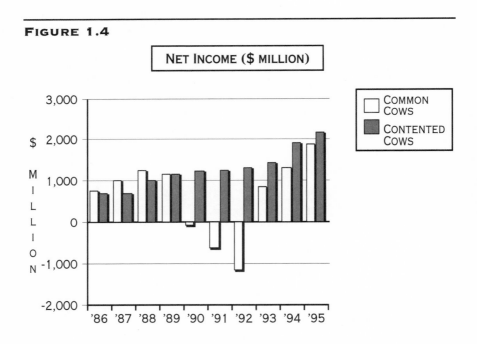

NET INCOME ($ MILLION)

6. Of much greater significance is the fact that, in raw dollars, the *Contented Cows* outearned the *Common Cows* by nearly $40 billion over the 10-year period. Earnings of the average *Contented Cow* company were roughly double those of their *Common* counterparts. (See Figure 1.5)

COMPANY	10 YR. NET INCOME ($ MILLION)	COMPANY	10 YR. NET INCOME ($ MILLION)
GE	42,071	GM	21,035
LUV	881	UAL	576
MMM	11,351	XRX	4,780
FDX	1,334	CNF	382
HWP	10,057	TXN	3,046
WMT	13,226	S	9,841
TOTAL	78,920	TOTAL	39,660
AVG.	13,153	AVG.	6,610

Source: Moody's

FIGURE 1.5

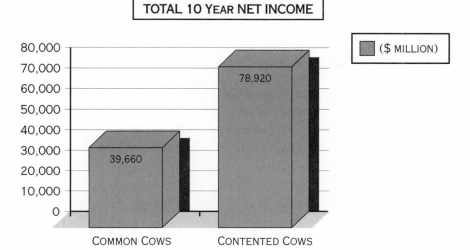

7. On a per-employee basis, as shown in Figure 1.6A and B, the *Contented Cows* again substantially outperformed their counterparts.

FIGURE 1.6A

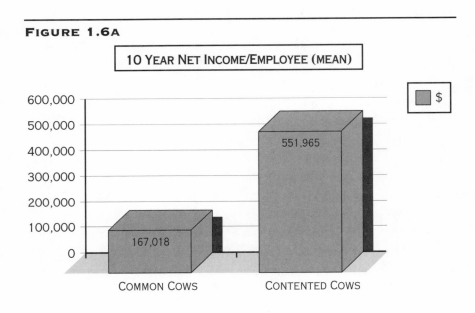

FIGURE 1.6B

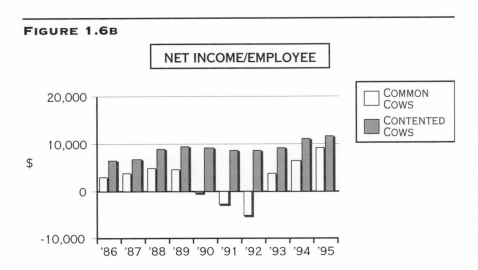

Here again, it's not just a matter of averages. In all six cases, the *Contented Cows* positively outmilked their competitors when it came to net income per employee, outearning them by a factor of three.

COMPANY	10 YEAR NET INC. PER EMPL. (MEAN)	COMPANY	10 YEAR NET INC. PER EMPL. (MEAN)
GE	151,662	GM	27,881
LUV	82,144	UAL	7,788
MMM	134,471	XRX	47,824
FDX	18,225	CNF	12,431
HWP	109,733	TXN	45,221
WMT	41,267	S	24,708

The "net income per employee" case is even more impressive when one considers the fact that over the 10-year period, the *Contented Cow* companies generated an average of 79,000 new jobs per company while the *Common Cows lost* on average 61,000! .

FIGURE 1.7

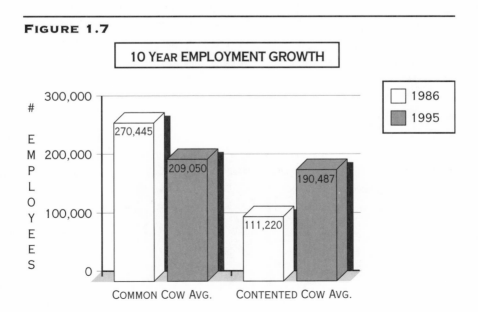

A "Head-to-Head" Comparison

Perhaps nowhere are the comparisons more stark than in the transportation sector. Carrying both human cargo and packages, four of the 12 companies do business in that sector, competing on a head-to-head basis.

Some might argue that the Federal Express vs. Consolidated Freight comparison is unfair because FedEx operates predominantly in the high priority end of the market. Yet, consider the fact that Emery Worldwide (owned by CF since 1989) not only was in that business, but dominated it before FedEx founder and CEO Fred Smith ever went to business school! So what was it that propelled FedEx to an average annual sales growth of 26 percent compared to CF's 14.9 percent and provided a net income per employee of $18,225 to CF's $12,431?

In all six cases, the Contented Cows positively outmilked their competitors when it came to Net Income per Employee, outearning them by a factor of three.

Southwest Airlines provides yet another clear-cut example. Relative to their competitors (not just United), they have fewer total employees per aircraft (79 versus 131); carry more passengers per employee (2,318 versus 848); have more available "seat miles" per employee (1,891,082 versus 1,339,995); enjoy a better reputation with their customers; and oh, by the way, they make more money.

How? In view of the fact that the regulations and capital costs under which each operates are nearly identical—planes are planes, trucks are trucks, fares are fares, routes are routes—the whole milking match pretty well comes down to whether or not "my people can outshoot and out-move yours."

MOVE IT OR LOSE IT

Consider the case of now defunct Eastern Airlines. Throughout most of its history as a commercial airline, Eastern competed on a head-to-head basis with Delta Air Lines. At one time during the competitive struggle between the two air carriers, the overlap of the markets they served approached 70 percent. Despite flying the same type aircraft (primarily mid-size Boeings and DC-9s) to the same cities, charging the same fares, and serving the same lousy food, one company died a very slow, painful death, and the other survived. What made the difference?

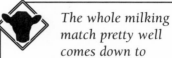

The whole milking match pretty well comes down to whether or not "my people can outshoot and out-move yours."

Well, in the case of Delta, their people were free to focus on attending to nothing but *customer* needs, secure in the knowledge that they were going to be treated fairly and respectfully by the company and their managers. In 1981, a fully engaged Delta workforce decided to chip in and buy the company a little present—a Boeing 767 jet! Conversely, at Eastern, employees were so balled-up worrying about their own work-related problems that they had precious little time, energy, or inclination to attend to the needs of paying customers.

THE SKYJACKED LUNCH

Noted author and consultant Charles Garfield tells a story which makes the point crystal clear. It seems that Garfield was on a lengthy, four-hour Eastern flight one day when a flight attendant approached his first class seat during the meal service with the news that she had run out of entrees—not just his preferred entree, but *all* of them. Despite having been hungry even before boarding the plane, and the fact that his nearest food was now several more hours away, Garfield decided to make the best of a bad situation by immersing himself in his work. His seatmate, on the other hand, apparently went "postal" over the matter, berating the airline, the flight attendants, and making all the usual threats.

After a while, Garfield got up to stretch and visit the restroom. On the way, he passed the galley, which had the curtains drawn around it. Deciding to stop and offer the flight attendants some consolation over his neighbor's rudeness, Garfield drew aside the curtains and found, to his amazement, two flight attendants consuming his and his seatmate's meals! At which point, one of them remarked, "Well, we've got to eat too, you know."[9]

THEY LOVE TO SMILE AND IT SHOWS

Around that same time, I* made a trip from Memphis to Salt Lake City on Delta. In Dallas, I boarded a packed 727 along with about 130 other souls. There was not an empty seat. With temperatures approaching 100 degrees, we sat on the plane for over an hour due to air traffic control delays. During that time, many passengers missed their connecting flights in Salt Lake City. We were not what you would call a happy bunch of people.

Midway into the flight, I was struck by the fact that, despite physical discomfort and personal inconvenience, the whole tenor of the people on the plane had changed from one of extreme agitation to a pleasant calm. Knowing they hadn't rolled a free booze cart down the aisle, I couldn't figure out what had caused the change. Then at one point during the meal service, I looked up and there stood all three flight attendants poised over passengers with meal trays—SMILING! These three women had accomplished with smiles what a fistful of free drink coupons and a rash of apologies could have *never* done.

Returning from the same trip a few days later, my flight was one of the last passenger flights to arrive that evening; the airline counters were all closed and the airport was deserted. I realized that I was well short of the amount of cash required to

---

* Authors' Note: Assuming the reader to be indifferent when it comes to the details of our personal lives, we have refrained from inserting ourselves into the narrative by not attributing anecdotes to either one of us. It suffices to say that no matter whose story it may be, we both agree on the lesson drawn from it.

retrieve my car from the parking garage. (They didn't accept credit cards, and my ATM card was elsewhere.) On the way to baggage claim, I happened into a fellow in a Delta uniform, a counter agent by the name of Boyd Collins. I introduced myself, told him about my problem, and asked if there was any way he could help me get a check cashed. Boyd explained that since the Delta counter was closed, and the cash had been locked up for the evening, his company couldn't do much for me. My heart sank momentarily. Then, without hesitation, he reached for his wallet, pulled out $50 of his own money, and said he'd be happy to cash my check.

Now some may argue that these two situations were highly unusual. Garfield happened to be on a flight with a couple of flight attendants who, for one reason or another, were just having a bad day, while I simply got lucky and stumbled into the equivalent of Santa Claus. Don't believe it. Anyone who has flown enough to know the difference between an aisle and a center seat knows better. The acts of these employees were *fully* representative of their respective organizations at the time.*

THE CORE OF OUR PHILOSOPHY

Before going further, let's get something straight. Our message concerning enlightened employee relations has nothing whatsoever to do with social or humanitarian interests. Instead, it's all about capitalism, pure and simple.

Or as Jim Barksdale, former chief operating officer of Federal Express and the current CEO of

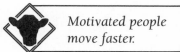

Motivated people move faster.

---

*It's ironic perhaps that Delta has of late flirted with some of the same destructive behavior that led to the undoing of first Eastern and later Texas Air. Caught in a vise created by a rapidly changing air transport market and the need to reduce operating expenses, the company has seemingly lost its way. In the process, a once proud workforce has grown increasingly dispirited and confused as the company's long standing "no furlough covenant" has been shaken, if not shattered, and the organization struggles with its identity. Do they want to be a no frills discount carrier a-la ValuJet, or a "real" airline? To some degree admitting the problem, then CEO Ron Allen said, "In some cases, we did cut too deeply." See *Business Week* (1/20/97), p. 30. Let's hope they get it figured out before they too pay the price.

Netscape, put it when describing the underlying rationale for the people philosophy at FedEx, "Motivated people move faster. Our people philosophy is not out of a spirit of altruism. You have fewer problems and make more money."[10] Charles Hampden-Turner of the London Business School puts it another way: "It's not just wrong to exploit workers, it's stupid. ... The trouble with crushing workers is that then you have to try to make high quality products with crushed people."

We'll say it again. What we are advocating is not the advancement of any social or humanitarian cause, but capitalism at its very best. Are the concepts of satisfied people and capitalism mutually exclusive? Of course not! In fact, they are inextricably linked.

> *Our message concerning enlightened employee relations has nothing whatsoever to do with social or humanitarian interests.*

There are those, however, who report to work each morning reciting a mantra which goes a little like this: "We're here for one reason and one reason only—to enhance shareholder wealth," and that's okay. But in our view, a problem emerges when that laudable goal is allowed to become the narrow, or even exclusive, focus of attention. To wit, the organization may actually be precluded from doing certain things, which in the long run, would otherwise best serve shareholder interests.

Levi Strauss CEO Robert Haas apparently agrees. "Everyone looks at the wrong end of the telescope, as if profits drive the business. Financial reporting doesn't get to the real stuff—employee morale, turnover, consumer satisfaction, on-time delivery, consumer attitudes, perceptions of the brand, purchase intentions—that drives financial results."[11]

YOUR REPUTATION IS WORTH MORE THAN YOU THINK

What is your reputation as an employer worth? What sort of things should you be doing to maintain and enhance that reputation? Organizations which don't measure up tend to be viewed as an employer of last resort; nobody with any brains, ability, or motivation wants to work there! When this occurs, only two things can happen. Either the organization is forced to pay market-premium wages and salaries in an attempt to secure better applicants, or it must accept the lower quality applicants, or do both. And, while the impact of bad hiring won't show up in the earnings for this quarter or next, rest assured it *will* show up.

One *very* capitalistic organization that has taken this lesson to heart is GE. At one time GE had a somewhat less-than-sterling reputation as an employer, and the company suffered because of it. However, due in large part to Jack Welch's leadership, the company has steadily worked its way back. Having re-established its reputation as an excellent place to work, GE has become a targeted destination for some of the very best and brightest folks in business. They've managed to recruit one of the "deepest benches" anywhere in the corporate world. To those who might say "so what?" consider these questions: If GE, and others like them have talented people begging and practically fighting to go to work there, do you suppose their managers find the task of recruiting easier or harder? Do they have to pay people relatively more, or less to work there? Now contrast that with your own situation, and a 1996 Conference Board study reflecting that 43 percent of companies surveyed reported problems finding and keeping high-quality workers.

Organizations which don't measure up tend to be viewed as an employer of last resort; nobody with any brains, ability, or motivation wants to work there!

PRAGMATIC IDEALS

If we boil all this down, what remains is a set of beliefs and practices driven by a great sense of pragmatism. According to Haas, "I believe that if you create an environment that your people identify with, that is responsive to their sense of values, justice, fairness, ethics, compassion, and appreciation, they will help you be successful. There's no guarantee—but I will stake all my chips on this vision."[12] Look at what works, and emulate it.

Lands' End President and CEO Mike Smith summed it up for us in the following note:

The title of your book would create a few smiles and knowing nods of the head among our agricultural neighbors here in Dodgeville, Wisconsin, as well as among the majority of our Lands' End Employees. Although it's difficult to give you the bottom line in dollars and cents ... I can relate some examples that may help.

Our retention rate for hourly and salaried positions is extremely high. That creates costs savings in recruiting, hiring, and training for us. With over 3,000 employees in these positions, there is a substantial savings here.

We have been ranked as one of the 100 Best Companies to Work For in America. Our pride in our work and friendliness received the highest ratings. This turns into recruitment savings by having a culture that people look for and that our own employees refer qualified candidates to. The effect is a top quality candidate pool combined with the previously mentioned retention which results in a great work force.

Our employee friendliness directly affects our customers, resulting in high customer satisfaction. We receive thousands of customer letters annually that reflect how much they appreciate our quality products and our service level. This definitely has a bottom line impact ...

Sincerely,

Mike Smith
President and CEO, Lands' End

So why not do what Lands' End, GE, Levi Strauss, and other employers of choice have done? Build an organization full of capitalists—people with pride and a critical stake in the enterprise. Try to look at the situation logically. If management wants one thing, and employees want the opposite, it's a simple high school physics problem. There's more of them than there are of you, and the side with the most mass and energy is going to prevail. For as long as this goal incongruence exists, each side is going to spend its time accumulating or withholding energy rather than being productive. In the end, everybody loses.

Faced in the '80s with the entry of UPS into the next-day priority air express market, FedEx applied this lesson in a big way. Wanting to make United Parcel's debut as painful and expensive as possible, the company contemplated "raising the bar" by changing the next-day service standard on delivery commitments from noon to 10:30 A.M. The 90-minute difference doesn't seem like much until you consider that it represented about a 40 percent reduction in the time available for sorting somewhere on the order of a million packages each night.

Time and again the company's planners and industrial engineers calculated the number of additional package handlers and sorters they would need to hire in order to pull it off, and each time it added up to a financial disaster. Finally, Hub Operations Vice President Karl Birkholz—who will likely forget more about discretionary effort and goal congruence than Elton Mayo ever knew—proposed that what they really needed to do in order to "help the python choke down this pig" was to rework "the deal" for his 3,000 or so college-aged, hourly paid, part-time employees whose job it was to sort all those packages.

> *If management wants one thing, and employees want the opposite, it's a simple high-school physics problem.*

Recognizing that the company's objective (getting the packages sorted and the planes out quicker) and his employees' objective (making more money) were fundamentally at odds, Birkholz simply proposed giving his workers a minimum weekly hours guarantee that would allow them to go home (with pay) when their work was done. The company enacted the scheme and productivity went through the roof, allowing FedEx to profitably blunt their new competitor's foray into the overnight express market.

Care of the cow brings good fortune.[13]

—I Ching, or Book of Changes

CONTENTED COWS: A HISTORICAL PERSPECTIVE

ROBERT OWEN AND SCOTTISH MILLWORKERS

The concept of *Contented Cows* is certainly not new. It has some impressive historical precedent both in the United States and abroad. Even in cases where the concept's application has been flawed (and there have been several), it teaches us valuable lessons.

For the first quarter of the 19th century, Robert Owen owned and operated a highly successful cotton mill at New Lanark, in southwestern Scotland. Before you get visions of kilted lads and lassies frolicking in the heather, you should know that to work in a factory during Britain's industrial revolution was no day at the loch. At the time, Scotland's industrial belt was home to poverty, backbreaking labor, and deplorable working conditions. But Owen believed that one's character was a product both of inherited nature and of one's environment. Knowing he could do nothing to affect the former, he conducted an experiment in the latter, and created for a time, one of Britain's most flourishing and profitable corporations—with a large labor force enjoying working conditions far surpassing the low standards of that era.

Owen inherited a population of just under a thousand demoralized, unproductive workers. Gradually, he turned it into a group of 2,500 industrious and—compared to most of their fellow countrypersons—relatively satisfied members of society. He accomplished this feat by creating a work climate more conducive to human effort, and then gradually enriching the pot.

While his competitors worked their people 13 to 14 hours a day, the beneficent Owen required only 10½ hours a day from the adults in the mill, and less than that from the children! (When they weren't working, they attended the schools he had built for them.) While even those hours seem draconian by today's standards, it was a groundbreaking development in early Victorian Britain.

Turnover was a problem for Owen's contemporaries. Not so much because workers quit, but because they had the annoying habit of dying, often in their thirties. Although there was not much field research on which Owen could base his hypothesis, he theorized that creating a community in which workers could live to a ripe old age and focus their energy on their work, rather than their problems, could only bring in more profits for him and his partner. His theory proved to be valid and, for more than a generation, made him a wealthy man.

The milltown, beautifully preserved today as a popular attraction on the banks of the River Clyde, near Glasgow, promised not only humane treatment of workers and more reasonable working conditions, but featured a strong emphasis on education. All employees' children, from the age of 2, were enrolled in superior schools in the village. Shopping, healthcare, and even social outlets and recreation were provided, all without leaving New Lanark.

What motivated Robert Owen? From the outset, he seemed very much a capitalist. He figured that workers distracted by trying to survive couldn't possibly produce as much for him as people who at least had a fighting chance of attending to their own basic needs. Even Frederick Engels, unabashed socialist and coauthor of the infamous *Communist Manifesto*, said that Owen's philosophy and practices were "based upon this purely business foundation, the outcome, so to say, of commercial calculation. Throughout, [his practices] maintained this practical character."[14]*

---

*In later years, Owen lost sight of the pragmatism that Engels recognized in him, became preoccupied with developing a utopian society, and screwed the whole thing up. Eventually, social idealism overtook the straightforward, practical ideology on which New Lanark was founded, and the community, along with its American counterpart, New Harmony, Indiana (also established by Owen), failed. Both communities stopped emphasizing the honor of labor, and the paternalism that evolved in its place attracted loafers and bums who liked the idea of being taken care of. See Cliff Hanley, *History of Scotland* (Gallery Books, 1986), p. 98.

MILTON HERSHEY AND THE TOWN
THAT CHOCOLATE BUILT

A century later, another pragmatist built a community, one which remains today—a community built of chocolate. Milton S. Hershey stumbled onto candy making after a series of small enterprises collapsed behind him. He literally went from rags to riches in four short years, and in the process, built the town of Hershey, Pennsylvania. Some said his success was due to his willingness to peel off his coat and work beside any of his workers any time. Others said it was the candy maker's motto, "Stick to it." Still others attributed his company's explosive and then sustained growth to Hershey's recognition that if you take care of certain basic needs for people so they can concentrate on their work, they'll make money for you. (As evidenced by Hershey's rank on Stern Stewart's MVA list—140th in 1996, with MVA of $3.4 billion—they've done quite well in this regard.)[15]

Hershey's practical approach to the business he built emanated not so much from ideology, but from necessity. When he decided to build a chocolate factory, he couldn't afford to buy land in the more developed areas of his homestate of Pennsylvania, but the price of land in the central part of the state was very attractive. There was only one problem; nobody lived out there. Undaunted, Hershey built not only a chocolate plant, but an entire town. He made housing available, put in schools, a bank, hotel (stay there if you ever have the chance), churches, parks, golf courses, and a zoo. He even installed an extensive trolley system to provide transportation for those who settled in the new town of Hershey. During the Great Depression, rather than laying off and retrenching, Hershey hired and grew.

RUMINATE ON THIS

Look, we're not pushing any kind of idyllic society. Far from it. Times have changed, and a company's practices must reflect its operating environment. In Victorian Scotland, people needed shelter, medicine, hours that wouldn't kill them, and education for their children. And crass as it may sound, Robert Owen knew that every young widowed mother mourning the premature death of her husband represented another fully consuming but unproductive member of society. His plan simply gave people more of what helped them and less of what dragged them down.

Similarly, Milton Hershey wasn't interested in offering his chocolatiers a sweet deal at his expense. In his time and place, the only affordable option meant going to the frontier. His plan would work only if he could provide productive workers with a town, or at least a way to get to the factory. Otherwise, who would make the chocolate?

When people are afforded the opportunity to focus freely on their work, and that opportunity is backed by high expectations and appropriate rewards, they'll—guess what?—do their jobs. It's very much in your self interest to create and support a satisfied workforce, because that workforce can build wealth almost as fast as a disgruntled one can destroy it.

Ultimately, the whole thing comes down to the same factors which motivated Fred Smith's pilots at FedEx to gas up company jets with their personal credit cards. Or moved Delta's employees to buy the company an airplane, while Eastern's flight attendants were busily stuffing their faces with food intended for passengers.

Contented Cows do give better milk, and better milk translates to better profits. Period. As we continue to make the case with cold, hard facts, and analyze what it takes to create and maintain a capably led, satisfied, highly motivated workforce, expect some holes to be poked in the myths that abound about what employee satisfaction *really* is. We're willing to bet it's probably not what you think.

CHAPTER SUMMARY

1. Productivity comes from people, not machines.

2. The notion of *Contented Cows* is anything but new—we've known for a long time that people can choose to contribute if they *want* to.

3. People factors are a source of competitive advantage or disadvantage; the choice is yours.

4. Over a 10-year period, the *Contented Cow* companies:

   a. Outgrew the *Common Cows* by a 4:1 margin and $111,000 per employee.

   b. Outearned them by nearly $40 billion and $384,000 per employee.

   c. Generated a net difference of better than 800,000 jobs.

5. MVA and EVA evidence is hard to argue with.

6. The argument is for capitalism, not cynicism or humanism.

COWS WITH ATTITUDE

You can make a happy person into a good worker, but not necessarily the other way around.

—Gordon Segal – founder, Crate & Barrel

WHERE DOES CONTENTMENT BEGIN?

We have a healthy suspicion that under your breath right now, you might be muttering things like, "Let's dispense with all this idealistic happy-go-lucky stuff. My employees are what they are. Some of them enjoy working here and give every appearance of being energized by their work, and others don't. They're just not contentable, and I don't see that changing!" You could well be right.

Let's clarify something. The job of "morale maintenance" in your organization does *not* rest entirely on your shoulders, or the shoulders of management in general. But, you'll produce better results if you take reasonable steps that *are* well within your grasp to promote workplace satisfaction.

Managers face at least three challenges with respect to employee motivation and satisfaction (ALL of which involve basic questions about human psychology and its relationship to morale):

1. Hiring people who have the potential to be both productive and satisfied in your specific environment.

2. Turning the boat around if the majority of the people at work are, shall we say, less than ecstatic already. One way or another, you *do* have to play the hand you were dealt.
3. Keeping them on track once you get them there.

> *The job of "morale maintenance" in your organization does not rest entirely on your shoulders, or the shoulders of management in general.*

Do companies see people on the asset or the liability side of the balance sheet? Are employees an opportunity—a source of strategic advantage—or a cost to be reckoned with, and minimized whenever possible? Sadly, most economic and planning models seem to be front-loaded with the assumption that people don't want to work, and won't work without costly stimuli.

PEACH LIMBS DON'T GROW ON OAKS

A major assumption operating in most businesses is that they exist to make a profit. (At least we know it is in ours.) Hence, almost all of our behavior is in response to that assumption. If we're going to discuss the kinds of practices that will transform your business into a grass-bellied, milk-producing, *Contented Cow*, we first have to deal with the assumptions on which your company operates.

The Coaching Skills training we provide for managers is based in part on the notion that, in order to become more productive, the boss/subordinate relationship needs to be put on more mature footing. Unfortunately, in some organizations, the managerial mindset is still anchored by some deep authoritarian roots; to wit, the change effort is almost certain to fail.

For your practices to be sustainable over time, they must line up with your assumptions. Roosevelt Thomas, founder of

Atlanta's American Institute for Managing Diversity, said it quite succinctly, "Peach limbs don't grow on oaks."[1] He was referring to the fact that a peach limb grafted onto an oak tree will appear to live for a brief time, only to soon die and fall off. You can fake practices you don't believe in for a while, but over the long haul, you won't be able to pull it off.

If you change your employee relations practices without examining the assumptions that drive them, you're certain to be disappointed. In all likelihood, those changes will be arbitrary, weakly executed, short-lived, ineffective, and, worst of all, costly.

> *Fortunately, even when cows are left up to their own devices, they seldom develop poor temperament and vices.*[2]
> —Improving the Welfare of Dairy Cows Through Management

YOU GET WHAT YOU EXPECT TO GET

So, what do you assume about the people who work in your organization or team? What do you assume about people in general?

If you believe that most people who come to work for you are lazy, stupid, untrustworthy, inept, and just downright contrary, that assumption can't help but show up in the way you run your business. You'll have all kinds of rules and regulations designed for numbskulls who couldn't pour milk out of a boot with the directions printed on the heel. You'll no doubt have a supervisor for every six or seven folks, and will inevitably attract just the kind of people who will live down to your assumptions. Discerning, competent employees won't come anywhere near your place, and your original assumption about people will be reinforced. If you are getting dizzy from the circular nature of all this, let's provide a real, albeit ultra-simple, example.

A CONSPIRACY AT THE DRY CLEANERS

Prominently displayed on the wall above the phone at my dry cleaners, in full view of everyone, is the following sign:

> **THIS PHONE IS NOT TO BE USED BY ANYONE FOR ANY REASON**
>
> **THE MANAGEMENT**

One day, being a rather curious sort, I asked one of the employees just what the sign was all about. As has happened on more than one occasion in my adult life, I got that I-can't-believe-you're-asking-such-a-stupid-question look. When pressed for a response, the counter clerk informed me that she had been told in no uncertain terms by the owner, a fellow named Paul, that the sign "meant exactly what it said."

So, I asked another question, "Then why do you have the phone?" Her reply was to the effect that the phone was only to be used for receiving inbound calls from customers. "Do you get many of those calls?" I asked. She indicated that there were only two to three of them per day. And the majority of those calls were from Paul's wife, who, in her words, was "keeping tabs on her husband."

"Then why the rule?" I had to ask.

"I don't know," she said. "I guess Paul doesn't trust us. And I don't know why not."

Which led to my final question. "If I asked to use the phone right now, would you let me?"

"Sure, I don't care. Paul's a jerk, and besides, he's not here now anyhow."

This is a minor example to be sure, but it serves to make a point. You are likely to get just the kind of behavior from employees that you expect. They will either live up or down to your expectations *because* your policies, procedures, and employment practices had at their bedrock those same assumptions.

I'm not going to have the monkeys running the zoo.[3]
—Frank Borman, former chairman of Eastern Airlines

CORE COVENANTS

Organizations operate on a limited number—not a great long list—of core beliefs and assumptions which are burned in to the very fabric of the business. Here are a few you should adopt (seriously) and begin operating on, today.

1. The Rule of Common Purpose: The organization must be managed in a way that permits all legitimate stakeholders—managers, employees, owners, and customers to benefit, each in their own way.

2. The Rule of Selective Membership: Since the beginning of time, winning organizations the world over have recognized and held dear the notion that membership is a privilege, and not a right. Contrary to popular belief, there really is an ample supply of conscientious, hardworking, capable, honest people. No doubt some of them already work for you. You can (and must) find others like them. You've got to expend a little effort doing it because "eagles don't flock," but they *are* out there. (If you can't accept this notion, sell your business to someone who can, or shut it down now!)

3. The Rule of Omission: In the main, your employees, customers, and yes, owners, will be inspired less by what you do *for* them, than by what you *don't* do *to* them. If, for example, you expect them to believe in you and stick with you, never, ever, ever deceive or abuse them! If the company conducts its business in a way that is *sufficiently satisfactory* (you don't have to be Mr. Wonderful) to the people who work there, most of them will perform better, producing more and better stuff.

BOGUS ASSUMPTIONS

Unfortunately, we have seen too many organizations operating on one or more of the following very erroneous and dangerous assumptions. Watch out!

- That people need paternalistic employers who will take care of them, because they are incapable of taking care of themselves.
- That the more we give people, without expecting anything in return, the happier and better off they'll be.
- That if we run a "kinder, gentler" organization, it will foster love, siblinghood, peace, goodwill, and the world will be a better place to live.

ASSUMPTIONS ARE A TWO-WAY STREET: THE EMPLOYEES' PERSPECTIVE

The whole subject of assumptions would simplify itself immensely if you only had to mind your own. The problem is everyone else has a set, too. Equally as important as your assumptions about your workforce is the whole question of *their* operative assumptions—about work, the organization, and about you personally.

For example, what are their assumptions about profit? How much is there? Where does it comes from? Where does it go? Given the continuing erosion of the trust factor in the workplace, what are their assumptions when they show up for work in the morning? Are they fully engaged? Or is it more like, "I know they're out to screw me, so I'll get them first?" Do you even know?

What are their assumptions about the organization's priorities right now? Have they had to figure this one out on their own? Or have you told them? Are you sure?

What are their assumptions about you? What's important to you? What do you stand for? Believe in? What will or won't you tolerate? Yes, we know. You probably told everyone this stuff when you hired them, right? But how long ago was that, and have your actions really been consistent with those statements made so long ago?

Unless you and your entire management team have invested considerable personal time and effort communicating honestly and openly—sharing the bad news as well as the good, showing people the numbers, helping them understand them, and making sure that your words are backed up by your actions—you've got people operating with bad data. In other words, your organization very well could be afflicted with a bad case of ignorance, curable, but ignorance nonetheless.

WHAT EMPLOYEES WANT—THE CONTENTED COWS' VIEW

The view taken by the *Contented Cow* companies seems to be that their employees want (and deserve):

1. **Meaningful Work** – Employees need to feel proud of their work. They want suitable challenges and the freedom to pursue them. They want to be in the game, not on the bench.
2. **High Standards** – They dislike losing organizations and don't want to hang around with losers.
3. **A Clear Sense of Purpose and Direction** – They want to read mysteries, not live them. Timely, relevant, and meaningful (truthful) information is a must.
4. **Balanced "Worth-its"** – A commensurate level of interest and investment in them must be demonstrated. Internal systems which support rather than impede their efforts. Freedom to pursue some things that are important to them.

5. **A Level Playing Field** – Means reciprocal caring, coupled with some sense of justice and an assurance they won't be taken advantage of.
6. **To Be and Feel Competent** – We don't need to explain this one, do we?

The "Happy Curve"

Most of this book deals with what happens to people at work, the way they're treated, regarded, related to, and enrolled in the organization's journey. But it's only fair to devote a little attention to a discussion of the importance of "contentability"—the *capacity to be contented.* None of the other ideas and examples we talk about will be of much benefit if you've managed to surround yourself with a herd of irascible beasts.

In an article published in *Business Horizons*, writer Dennis Organ advanced the theory that workplace morale depends not only on the work environment, but to some degree on the internal sense of happiness that employees possess or lack. In other words, hiring inherently happy people can exponentially boost the morale of the organization as a whole.[4]

We think it's a given that to have contented employees, you have to start with "contentable" ones. We've all known people who seem to be happy no matter what, and a few who aren't happy with anything. (For those in the latter category, the organization represents just one more thing to be unhappy about.) So, does job satisfaction depend on what happens to us at work? How we are treated? The so-called working conditions? Or is it an individual's emotional makeup? We think it's both.

Organ's story of Jack Davis makes an interesting case. A former corporate executive, Davis unscientifically formulated the idea of what he called the "Happy Curve," and then came upon some factual basis to back up what he had already figured out intuitively.

First, he noticed that a friend, usually a happy-go-lucky type, seemed to be down in the dumps. One day Davis sat down and talked with him, offering an understanding shoulder and a little encouraging advice. The friend went away refreshed, armed with a few new ideas, and a healthier perspective. It didn't take much to get him back in the saddle. Both knew it would end that way. The friend was just that kind of guy—normally happy, creative, energetic, and lots of fun. He was merely in a slump and needed a boost.[5]

Later, when he took over a company in crisis, Davis found himself with an abundance of opportunities to further test his theory of the "Happy Curve." A nightmare for shareholders, and a really bad place to work, most everyone was miserable, and with good reason. But not everyone. There was a small core of people who were up-beat, supportive, and optimistic, despite the problems around them.

Careful, deliberate observation of these people caused Davis and his staff (none of whom were trained psychologists) to conclude that these folks were just plain, cheerful people, on or off the job. They had stable, fulfilling family lives, interests outside of work, and were confident in their abilities. Ups and downs were a part of their lives too, but on balance, they liked themselves, and they stayed on an even, and relatively elevated, keel.[6]

Now consider the possibility, as Davis did, that each individual has a range of moods. "High" for one person may be "average" for another. Some people would never get as low as others. In fact, each person might have a sort of emotional "setpoint" (like the one that stabilizes our body weight) that their mood tends to gravitate toward, unless something really unusual is going on.[7]

Davis and his crew came to believe that they had somehow ended up with a disproportionately high number of people with relatively low Happy Curves.[8] In other words, the grouches had reached critical mass. Since morale is as much a group dynamic as an individual condition, the large share of low Happy Curves alone was enough to drag down some of the others at least a little.

As time passed, Davis made a conscious effort to hire people who not only were qualified, but seemed in general to have the potential for being happy. While no one was ever fired for being sullen (perhaps they should have been), the organization gradually took on a new, more positive outlook, sales improved, and the spiral turned upward.[9] Of course, higher morale was not the single "silver bullet" that saved this company, but it was an integral factor.

A STICKY VARIABLE

As it turns out, Davis' experience is corroborated by the results of a number of research studies. What we call "morale" is, according to University of California Berkeley professor Barry Staw, described as a "sticky" variable.[10] That means some of it is accounted for by what is innate about the person, as opposed to environmental factors.

For example, when organizational psychologists measure the job satisfaction of a group of people at two points in time separated by intervals of up to several years, the best and most consistent predictor of job satisfaction at the later time is the earlier assessment of job satisfaction. This finding holds up even when many people in the group have changed jobs or employers. A study of 5,000 adults begun in 1973 by the National Institute on Aging found that the happiest of people in that year were still relatively happy 10 years later, regardless of changes in their work or other circumstances.[11]

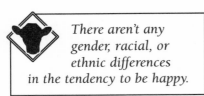

There aren't any gender, racial, or ethnic differences in the tendency to be happy.

Perhaps most telling, Staw and his research associates found that a high school counselor's rating of the "cheerfulness" of adolescents predicted their job satisfaction 30 years later as well or better than any single aspect of their jobs![12] Also persuasive are the results of studies of identical twins separated at birth, indicating that 30 percent or more of the variation in adult job satisfaction relates to genetic factors.[13] There might be something to this *sticky* variable business, but of course it's not the whole story. (And if you believe that 30 percent figure, we would guess that's not even half of it.)

We're not saying that work environment doesn't matter. You've had good jobs and bad ones, and you know there's a difference. But we think there's good reason to believe that people do vary in their tendencies to exhibit good morale, within a range, regardless of environmental factors. This in part explains why companies like Southwest Airlines "hire attitudes," preferring to train people in the skills they need. Unfortunately, you can't teach enthusiasm. Any company would do well to adopt a similar philosophy when recruiting.

Despite what you might have heard otherwise, you *can* hire "for fit" and still uphold your organization's commitment to equal employment opportunity. There aren't any gender, racial, or ethnic differences in the tendency to be happy. (The only acceptable discrimination in hiring practices should be directed against grouches!)

BUT WILL THEY BE CONTENTED HERE?

From the start, we have been making the case that *Contented Cows Give Better Milk*. It's an absolute fact. But it's also a fact that all cows aren't going to be content living on your ranch, so let's be truthful about it. By definition, the *Contented Cow* companies are viewed as exceptional places to work. But that holds true for only certain types of people, and *Contented Cows* unabashedly take steps to ensure that people who won't fit in with their particular environment don't go to work there. (And, if they do somehow manage to get on the payroll, that they don't last long!) In effect, what they are recognizing—and it's as true in your company as it is in theirs—is that not everyone would be happy, productive, or successful working there.

> *One measure of a person's capacity to be satisfied and productive at your company is the degree to which they can live with your ground rules.*

As you might guess, they employ a rigorous selection process. Hewlett-Packard candidates have been known to experience eight or more job interviews. Lincoln Electric, the decades-old Cleveland manufacturer of electric motors, reportedly takes it a step further by requiring every new hire to be interviewed and unanimously approved by a board of vice presidents and factory superintendents. Rick and Diane Ernst, who operate one of Alphagraphics' largest and most successful franchises go further still. After conducting an exhaustive recruiting and screening process, they pay potential hires $100 to work with their team

ALPHAGRAPHICS STORE LOCATIONS

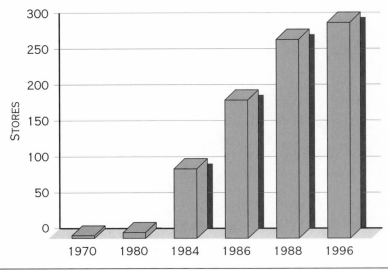

Source: Alphagraphics Company Spotlight, 1996

for a day; a measure which gives both parties the opportunity to make an informed decision and opt out, before it's too late. Such measures not only narrow the risk, but also make plain from the very start that the organization is deadly serious about employment matters. It also sends a message to the individual that he or she must be joining an elite organization, thus creating high expectations that in turn breed high performance.

One measure of a person's capacity to be satisfied and productive at your company is the degree to which they can live with your ground rules. Every organization has certain things which are in the realm of the sacrosanct. They are immutable. Changing them is not on the table for discussion. Among other things, *Contented Cow* companies realize the absolute futility of trying to convert someone whose internal compass points 40 degrees to the left of the corporation's. It's not a matter of morality, but makeup. More so than the average company, the *Contented Cow* companies have a crystal clear sense of direction and a keen awareness of their core values. Accordingly, they have little room for those who are unwilling to make the journey with them.

> *Many herds allow their cows to develop their own individual personali-*
> *ties as long as it does not mean special care and treatment. ... Individual*
> *cows must fit into the system rather than the system conforming to the*
> *habits of the cow.*
> —Improving the Welfare of Dairy Cows Through Management

CHICK-FIL-A: NEVER ON SUNDAY

You can't get a Chick-fil-A chicken sandwich, or anything else on the fast-service chain's menu on a Sunday, because each and every one of their stores is closed that day. If you want to know why, read founder Truett Cathy's book, *It's Easier to Succeed Than to Fail.*

In reality, it doesn't matter why. That's just the way they've chosen to run their business. It stands to reason that they could increase sales by opening their stores on Sunday, but if you want to do it that way, open a McDonald's franchise. Before you assume that they are too old-fashioned for their own good, consider the fact that the majority of Cathy's shopping center-based stores do more business in six days than their food court neighbors do in seven![14]

CHICK-FIL-A STORE LOCATIONS

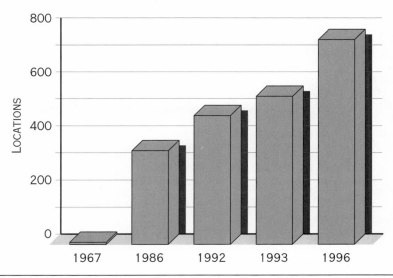

Source: Chick-fil-A Annual Message, 1997.

FedEx and Disney, on the other hand, are absolutely fanatical about their corporate appearance. Male applicants who choose to express their individuality by wearing a beard or earring, or women who wear heavy makeup and lots of jewelry shouldn't even slow down as they drive by the gates of either company. As former FedEx Vice President of Personnel Terry Bean used to put it when besieged by the "why can't we wear a beard?" question from the company's 60,000-plus customer contact employees: "You can wear a beard. You just can't do it and work here."

Disney was equally emphatic in 1991 in dealing with a strike by Disneyland employees over the same issue of facial hair. They fired the strike leader. The rest of the "cast" quickly came back to work, and the rule stayed. Any questions? The standards in both cases had been made impeccably clear from the beginning, before anybody was even hired. The company merely lived up to that standard.

For Miami Dolphins' Head Coach Jimmy Johnson, it's an individual's work ethic that counts as much (if not more) than speed or pass catching ability. Johnson has proven it several times over by trading or releasing outright some of the most talented players in the game. Do the names Herschel Walker and Bryan Cox ring a bell? Johnson cut them both loose. Certainly not because they couldn't play football, but because they lacked other essential requirements to play on his team. For Coach Johnson, a player has to be teachable; an unteachable player will be miserable personally and fail the team at crucial moments. Johnson amplifies the point in his book, *Turning the Thing Around*, "We evaluate a helluva lot more than vertical leap and 40-yard dash times. If I'm talking with a group of prospective draftees and one kid's sitting there flipping ice at his teammate, he'll be hard pressed to sit on my list for more than about five more minutes. I have formal training in the psychology of learning, but none of that does any good on an unwilling or uncaring pupil."[15]

Get good people and expect them to perform. Terminate them quickly and fairly if you make the wrong choice.[16]

—J. Willard Marriott, Jr.

Time after time, organization after organization, the winners are absolute zealots about who will and won't get to play on their team. At A.G. Edwards, according to CEO Ben Edwards, "We want someone with character who shares our values and who will fit into our culture. We're looking for a long term happy marriage."[17] More often than not, it's the intangible factors rather than raw credentials or ability they most rely on when making that decision. Chick-fil-A has a uniquely positive corporate culture. Operational expertise alone is not enough to cut it there. Truett Cathy says it's as much a person's character as anything else that he looks for when he hires an employee or contracts with an operator for one of his growing number of stores. For him, the fate of the applicant ultimately rests on a single consideration: "Would I like my son or daughter to work for this person?"[18] Their selectivity pays off in more ways than one. Their employee turnover rates, for example, consistently run at less than one-fifth the industry average. From now on, companies will need to reorient their recruitment and selection processes by hiring "for fit" rather than mere credentials or, for that matter, specific job openings.

CONTENTABILITY AND CORPORATE ASSIMILATION

We know what we've just advocated is that you hire only those people who will be able to *fit in* or assimilate to your culture. And we suspect you may have a problem with organizations that, at least in your eyes, impose "undue" requirements for assimilation. A requirement to assimilate can be a double-edged sword. When organizations require that people fit in around arbitrary or irrelevant considerations, they often filter out potential top performers who don't fit the irrelevant part of their mold. Whenever a company insists that a woman behave like "one of the guys," for example, or that people leave integral aspects of their identity at the door, they're putting the wrong filter on the selection process.

For example, is an inclination or ability to play golf a valid requirement for a job? Well, sure it is for some jobs, like a professional golfer, for instance! Or maybe for a sales position where lots of the company's customers like to do business on the golf course. Then the ability to play golf would be a pretty important job requirement.

I once consulted with a credit card company's vice president of marketing who was trying to pass a guy named Mike off to another department like a hot potato. Mike's "problem" was that he didn't "fit in" to the department. Of course he didn't fit in! Mike was a systems programmer whose job was to design and implement computer software for use by the marketing department. This guy got his kicks writing code in a foreign language and watching it turn into lights on a screen. He was a genius! He had developed some of the slickest stuff any of us had ever seen. Unmarried, he spent more than 60 hours at his terminal every week, both at the office and at home. I learned that the reason he didn't fit in was that he didn't drink and he didn't play golf. (*It's amazing how those two activities go hand-in-hand.*) Incredulous, I asked sarcastically, "What do you need, a wine-taster, or a computer guy!??" The veep was about to cast off one of his greatest assets, for a reason that amounted, in real terms, to nothing.

The other edge of this sword is that strong leaders of outstanding organizations realize that many people, regardless of talent, will not be able to meet the requirements necessary to succeed in their *Contented Cow* companies. It's not that they can't do the work, but that they won't be happy, productive, or successful working there. What sets these companies apart, though, is that they are actually doing something about the realization. Their assimilation criteria are strictly business-oriented, deliberate, and rational, and do not consist of conveniences, preferences, or unquestioned traditions.

To be sure, every organization requires some degree of assimilation. You must be completely in touch with the real requirements for success in your business, and highly disciplined in proclaiming those things loudly, clearly, and unashamedly to all who would invest their time and hopes in working there. Ultimately, as Roosevelt Thomas puts it, "There will always be a need for some assimilation. People will always have to salute certain organizational flags. The job of the leader is to be very clear about which flags need to be saluted."[19]

Company standards and assimilation criteria exist for a reason, and frequently, it begins with the letter "C," for Customer. Concerning the beard issue at FedEx, for example, the message they've gotten loud and clear from literally hundreds of focus group sessions with their customers is that they prefer a neatly attired, clean-cut look. The way the company sees it, as much money as you're paying to do business with them, they're only too happy to oblige.

Disney is every bit as emphatic about the use of coarse language. But if you fathom the simple logic behind Disney's requirement, it has a lot to do with the fact that the majority of what they sell is based on an image of clean, wholesome entertainment for some very impressionable kids.

It's no less the case at Marriott, where only about 10 percent of job applicants meet the company's requirements. If an applicant is at all uncomfortable with their clean-living, extremely service-conscious environment, he/she will not make it there. Some would say that the Marriott Way has its roots in the company's Mormon-influenced origins. Maybe so. But as frequent Marriott guests, we can tell you that wherever it comes from, it most assuredly makes a difference. Ditto for others like J&J, HP, Nordstrom, and Procter & Gamble.

THE PROOF IS IN THE PEOPLE

Having put forth some of the behavioral drivers behind the best stool-and-bucket *Contented Cow* companies, let's describe three very fundamental characteristics they share regarding their employment practices. Are you ready? The rest of this book is going to hang on these three branches (no speed-reading).

While the *Contented Cow* companies are unique in many ways, they share remarkable commonality in three important respects. Day in and day out, *each* of them does a remarkable job of:

1. Getting (and keeping) their people solidly lined up behind the organization's core purpose and objectives. In short, they're **Committed**.
2. Letting people know through a myriad of ways, some large (but mostly small), that they're important. They're more than just a number or body. They are **Cared About**: first as people, then as professionals.
3. Through personal as well as systemic means, removing the obstacles from the path of their workforce. In short, they have **Enabled** their people to perform.

Analyzing each of these areas in the chapters to come, we'll address the following questions:

1. What exactly are the components of these characteristics? How will you recognize it when you see them?
2. How can you replicate it? Here, we'll look at two aspects of the equation:
    a. Employee relations practices – These are obviously (we think they're obvious) those things you actually do to promote contentment and productivity. You know—pay, benefits, employee involvement, team-

work, the hiring and decision-making processes—all of them—and more.

b. Operational practices – All the decisions you make about running the business which aren't directed at employee relations—but that employees nonetheless must depend on or contend with. These are less obvious, because they won't come up in a discussion of employee relations, but they have a tremendous effect on contentedness, and on frustration levels. Things like customer service policies, safety, equipment maintenance, etc.

3. What are the employees' responsibilities? What must people do to ensure their own contentment? This is anything but a one-way street.

4. Finally, to help you three-dimensionalize the ideas governing each chapter, we'll identify some of the people and organizations that are doing an especially good job in these areas. From time to time, we'll also take a look at those which have "climbed the mountain" but, due to a failed strategy in other respects, have lost ground, money, or ceased to exist altogether.

Our job, then, will be to pick through the situations and examples, bringing to light those which define each characteristic in the simplest, clearest, and most replicable manner.

CHAPTER SUMMARY

1. Just as they affect virtually every other outcome in our lives, our assumptions about people (their relative good or bad qualities, and their propensity to work without first being threatened) drive our employee relations practices, and in turn, the outcome of the relationship. You get what you expect. Practices that are inconsistent with your organization's operating assumptions are doomed to fail.

2. Never lose sight, even for a moment, of the expectations of employees in a *Contented Cow* company, most notably their requirements for:
   - meaningful work
   - high standards
   - clear purpose and direction
   - balanced "worth-its"
   - a level playing field
   - being and feeling competent

3. Similarly, don't allow yourself to become distracted by the bogus assumptions that are often put before us, particularly those advocating "kinder and gentler" standards (or no standards at all); blatant paternalism; or the need to give or pay more without good and compelling reasons.

4. Hire "for fit," and not just talent. Make sure the *fit* requirements are relevant to business success.

5. Face it, not everyone's going to be content "living on your ranch."

6. Contented Cows are:
   - **Committed**
   - **Cared About**
   - **Enabled**

SECTION TWO

CONTENTED COWS ARE COMMITTED

THE "VISION THING" ... PASSENGERS OR CREW

It doesn't take a genius to figure out that in an environment where there is a shared vision of excellence ... where people can be the best they can be on a daily basis ... where, when they know what is expected of them ... understand that reward is linked to performance ... and BELIEVE they can make a difference because they will be heard ... they WILL make a difference. They will go BEYOND our expectations and great things will start to happen.[1]

—FedEx founder and CEO Frederick W. Smith

JUST ALONG FOR THE RIDE

Not long ago, we met with a business unit training manager for one of the world's largest telecommunications companies. This individual, who had expressed an interest in some of the training we do, had been with the company in the same location for 19 years and had worked in almost every staff department under the roof. Following our customary routine, we asked her, "What kind of training do you currently provide for the employees here?" Her answer, sounding like something straight out of a departmental policy manual was, "Oh, whatever kind of training they need to make and deliver our products." Because of the breadth and complexity of her company's operations (and the fact that this was our first meeting with her), it seemed reasonable to ask, "And what products do you make and deliver here?"

"I knew you were going to ask me that," she said. "To be honest with you, I couldn't tell you. I don't have any idea." Needless to say, we were more than a little dumbfounded to hear a 19-year veteran whose whole professional life had been with the same employer—which was not the CIA—admit to being totally ignorant about where her paycheck came from. How in the world can she possibly be contributing, let alone doing a good job? How can her daily actions result in anything other than an impediment to the organization's success? Some might suggest that this is such an extreme example as to border on the ridiculous. We'd like to believe that, but we're not so sure.

DESTINATION UNKNOWN?

Billions are spent every year on internal corporate communications, including $50 million-plus by the above-referenced company. Even so, most organizations still do a miserable job of helping their folks understand the direction, goals, and priorities of the business (let alone securing their Commitment to them). If you doubt the magnitude of this "failure to communicate" claim, take five minutes and go do some field research of your own. Ask a sample of your people to jot down what *they* believe to be the organization's three highest priorities and where they think it is headed. When the answers come back without any degree of consistency, the question is obvious: *If they don't know where you're going, how can they possibly help you get there?*

BURNING OFF THE FOG

Clearly, in some companies people seem to "get it," and in others they don't. We wanted to know what makes the difference. If your people know (*really* know) what the organization is all about, how did they find out? What did you have to do?

We asked these questions of almost everyone we came in contact with while writing this book. Aside from the fact that most leaders simply didn't have an answer, the few who did offered nothing terribly new or complicated. We had hoped to hear of some ingenious, idiot-proof techniques guaranteed to inject the milk of human understanding into every living thing under the corporate roof. We didn't find any. But what we *did* hear over and over from organizations whose people do seem to "get it" and "get it good" is that you simply tell them, and show them by practically "carpet bombing" people from day one with the same simple, clear-cut, credible message.

In a survey of senior executives at 86 major firms, respondents told Mercer Management Consulting, Inc. that half their employees couldn't even articulate the corporate strategy. (*We'd like to meet the half who could.*) Mercer's study found one reason for this shortcoming was that the business strategy and direction had been set at a level too far over the heads of people at the operating level. Any sense of ownership or degree of understanding on their part was virtually precluded.[2] We submit there are at least four more reasons which explain this phenomenon:

1. The Event Syndrome. In all too many cases, the attempt to communicate these priorities, goals, etc., takes place only once a year, or maybe every three or four years, usually after some mountain-top retreat or strategic planning session. A wonderfully crafted letter, speech, pamphlet, or video is produced. Everyone endures the obligatory viewing, and then promptly goes back to what they were doing, safely assured that the topic won't come up again for at least another year.

In one organization familiar to us, the senior management group returned from its three-day, mountain-top experience in "Moses-like" fashion, bearing (*get this*) stone tablets with the newly minted corporate goals inscribed on them. With phrases like "competitively superior, highly integrated, broad-based networks" inscribed on the tablets, we're fairly certain that more than a few of their people couldn't even pronounce some of this stuff, let alone understand or remember it. Fortunately, those rocks made pretty good paperweights.

2. Message of the Week. In other cases, companies somehow expect all those thoughtful, intelligent people they call employees to buy the notion that this week they're a "Market Leader," knowing all the while that next week they'll be the "Most Operationally Efficient," "Lowest Cost Producer," or something else. Come on, get real! It's almost as if many executives are suffering from the very same Attention Deficit Disorder that grips a lot of of our school-age children. (Maybe there should be a Ritalin Rx for the boardroom.)

3. **"Watch Their Bellybutton" or "Talk is Cheap."** Early in their careers, basketball players are taught that one of the best ways to anticipate movement when guarding an opponent is to watch their midsection, as it reliably predicts where the rest of the person is going. The same thing is true off the court, as well. Too often, what our people see is our bellybutton going one way and our mouth another.

4. **Mission Statement vs. Sense of Mission.** Comparatively speaking, executives spend entirely too much time and precious energy crafting precisely worded mission, vision, and value statements relative to the effort they invest in making darned sure every human being on their payroll truly understands and appreciates what all that stuff means.

> *Executives spend entirely too much time and precious energy crafting precisely worded mission, vision, and value statements relative to the effort they invest in making darned sure every human being on their payroll truly understands and appreciates what all that stuff means.*

In case after case, the *Contented Cow* companies are the ones doing the best job of helping their people see, feel, and appreciate where the business is headed, why it is going there, and what role they are expected to play. While their efforts aren't usually the slickest or fanciest (no stone tablets to be sure), they are clear, consistent, and "udderly" compelling.

A leader has got to show his troops the route of the march and the destination.[3]

—Frank Pacetta, Xerox Sales Manager

EYE ON RETAIL: WHAT HAPPENED?

It's impossible to talk about the retail sector without examples from companies like Wal-Mart and Sears—the really big merchandisers—dominating the discussion. While each operates in this brutally competitive arena, there are some distinct differences, both on and off the income statement. Together they accounted for $117 billion in combined annual revenues in 1995. However, as Figures 3.1 and 3.2 indicate, the commonality between them may end with the T-shirts, car batteries, and housewares which each of them sells.

While our intent is not to malign Sears (or any other company), the fact remains that they have had their problems, both in the boardroom and in their stores. Largely, these problems stemmed from an arrogance displayed toward both customers and employees, but not necessarily in that order. In 1989, Sears' Allstate Insurance unit (the "Good Hands People") effectively cratered relations with its sales force by unilaterally imposing de facto sales quotas—a move that spawned widespread defections, and, according to some, questionable underwriting practices. Ditto for its auto repair unit, where in the early '90s, a new compensation scheme sparked complaints of unnecessary repairs and

FIGURE 3.1

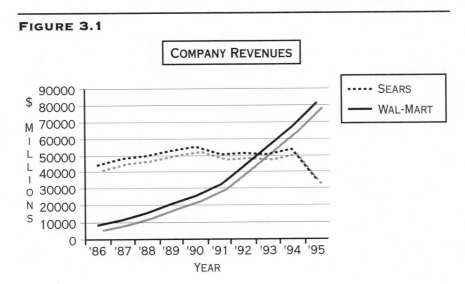

FIGURE 3.2

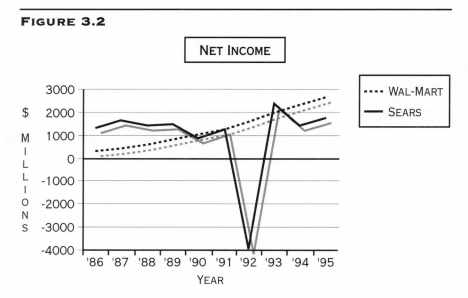

overcharges, causing the company to pay out millions to settle claims in California and New Jersey.[4]

Sears' inability to effectively decide, let alone communicate, what business it was in resulted in the closure or sale of its Coldwell Banker Real Estate operations, Dean Witter, Eye Care Centers of America, the Discover Card operations, Allstate, the venerable catalog (*America's Wish Book*), and associated catalog stores. Even the Sears Tower office building in Chicago. In the process, they whacked more than 100,000 heads from their payroll and left some 360,000 not especially happy people wondering who or what would be next.

Wal-Mart and J.C. Penney, on the other hand, have long been recognized as companies which go to great lengths to maintain a satisfied, highly motivated workforce. Both are well known for having straightforward business philosophies which they take pains to share with their workforce, along with a handsome share of the profits. Nowhere is this more evident than with the 622,000 Wal-Mart "associates" who participate regularly in a variety of meetings and special recognition events designed expressly to keep both them and company management informed about what's going on in the real world.

Keep in mind that communicating with the Wal-Mart workforce is no mean feat. First, as we have already mentioned, there are more than a half million people to communicate with. Second, consider the fact that their workforce is comprised largely of second career mothers, senior citizens, and teenagers. (Imagine trying to have a business-related conversation with *your* adolescent son or daughter.)

But communicate they do. According to the late Sam Walton, founder of Wal-Mart, "It all comes down to how well [we] can communicate and truly be sincere in helping [our] associates understand what our basic philosophy is, and what our

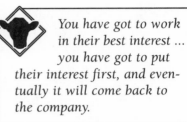

You have got to work in their best interest ... you have got to put their interest first, and eventually it will come back to the company.

basic goals are, and involving them in our business. ... I guess our greatest technique and our greatest accomplishment is this commitment to communicating with them in every way that we possibly can, and listening to them constantly. I think every good company has got to have that kind of aura, have a partnership relationship, really, with their employees. You have got to work in their best interest. ... You have got to put their interest first, and eventually it will come back to the company."5

GETTING THE CUSTOMER-FOR-LIFE TREATMENT

Walton is absolutely right. The demonstrated commitment does "come back to the company" through Wal-Mart employees like Lisa (not her real name), who works in the jewelry department of a store near my home. In search of a battery for my wife's watch, I stopped at Lisa's store after visiting Sears, where I had been shrugged off with a curt, "Nope, we don't have it. Nope, we don't carry the watch. Nope, we don't know where you can get one." (Sears originally started out as the R.W. Sears Watch company. Ironic, huh?)

Although Wal-Mart didn't have a new battery either, Lisa managed to find a used one with some charge left in a box of spare watch parts. Because the timepiece had been purchased elsewhere (Wal-Mart did not even carry the brand), Lisa informed me she'd be happy to give me the battery, but that I would have to install it myself. She was prohibited from working on watches the store didn't carry, just in case a repair went wrong and a replacement could not be offered. After watching all 10 of my thumbs struggling to crack open the back of this tiny ladies' dress watch and install a battery the size of a BB, Lisa cautiously but confidently intervened. She did what you should want your employees to do, even in the face of a policy to the contrary.

So, what was the net of this transaction? First, it would have been far easier and safer for Lisa to do nothing, like her Sears counterpart, rather than spend half an hour with someone not even making a purchase and defy a store policy in the process. Wal-Mart didn't recognize one dime in revenue from the deal *on that particular day*, but they did get what Texas car dealer Carl Sewell has termed a Customer for Life—a customer they will make plenty of money from over the years.

Perhaps the better question is *why* did this happen? What is it that Wal-Mart knows that Sears managed to forget in its storied 110-year past? Somehow, somewhere along the way, in a Wal-Mart store meeting, or one of those goofy pep rallies we've all heard about, or in the course of a conversation with her manager, or more probably *all* of the above, Lisa got the message that even at the ripe old age of 20, her opinion mattered. She was secure in the knowledge that as long as she was looking out for a customer and doing what she felt to be right, she was not only permitted but expected to use her own best judgment, *even if it meant contradicting a policy decree from some vice-president in Bentonville, Arkansas.* Her counterparts at Sears, on the other hand, had fallen victim to a culture so authoritarian that someone in Sears management actually felt they needed three pages of policy guidelines to clarify how and when people were to take coffee breaks![6]

MOMENTS OF TRUTH

In his 1987 book *Moments of Truth*, SAS Airline President Jan Carlzon suggested that it is in these fleeting moments of inter-action between customers and front-line employees that the fate of any customer-driven organization is determined. Speaking of SAS, he said, "If we are truly dedicated to orienting our company toward each customer's individual needs, then we cannot rely on rule books and instructions from distant corporate offices. We have to place responsibility for ideas, decisions, and actions with the people who are SAS during those brief seconds."[7]

To be sure, Carlzon was not advocating that businesses be run simply on the whims of whatever each individual employee happens to feel like doing at the moment. There needs to be some form of structure and decision-making process. But, like Sam Walton, he is suggesting that in many organizations the gulf that exists between a truly involved workforce hitting on all cylinders, and one that gives every appearance of being brain dead can be best bridged with credible information—artfully presented and continually reinforced—about **where** the organization is going, **why** it's going there, what it stands for, and **what** it needs and expects from all hands on deck. Good, timely information enables people to perform at a higher rate of speed and with fewer errors. Without that information, they must inevitably slow down to sort things out.

Walk into *The Sandwich Store*, a nondescript little deli in Jacksonville, Florida, and within nanoseconds you'll realize that you are in the presence of four people who are absolutely on a mission. That mission, which each of them has so clearly embraced, is to "serve lunch fast!" The food is good, very good, in fact, but what's really impressive is the speed with which Renee Curry, the thirtysomething owner of the shop, and her three co-workers can make a sandwich, fill a soft drink cup, ring up an order, get it all correct, and get people on their way somewhere between 300–400 times per day!

These folks are focused like a laser on that objective, and execute so well that we would highly recommend the place to the industrial engineers at McDonald's and Burger King who could no doubt learn a thing or two. Sometimes getting the message of "what we're all about" across to the troops is a simple matter of telling them clearly and showing them *consistently*. As Carlzon puts it, "Setting a good example is truly the most effective means of communication—and setting a poor one is disastrous!"[8] This is clearly a lesson not lost on Renee.

THERE IS NO SUCH THING AS OVER COMMUNICATION

In 1995, the Families and Work Institute conducted a survey in which they asked people, "Besides compensation, what else is important in your job?" The number one answer, besting such predictable responses as job security, nature of the work, and "my supervisor," was open communication.[9] People want you to tell them what they need to know to do their jobs.

We talked with David Graham, CEO of InTuition, Inc., a privately-held, 500-employee company that provides data and other services to the student loan industry. We wanted to find out how InTuition took a four million dollar loss in 1991—the year Graham and his partners took over the management of the company (which they later bought)—and turned the red ink into four million in profits five years later. Not surprisingly, his answer was "our people." But when we probed a little further, we found that this relatively small *Contented Cow* company really *had* been able to rebuild largely on the back of an inspired workforce.

From whence came the inspiration? Information. "Because we think it [communication] is so important," says Graham, "we've made it company policy to create as many opportunities and mechanisms for communication as possible. There's no such thing as over communication."[10]

At InTuition, communication starts with a three-day orientation. Normally, we are not big fans of orientations, at least in the traditional sense, because most of them have been reduced to mindless drivel and filling out forms. But we like what happens at InTuition's orientations and afterward. Together with COO Claude Collier, Graham talks with new hires about InTuition's relatively short but checkered history, its culture, and everyone's mutual expectations. Then, a few months later, they reassemble the orientation group for an "Orientation Reunion." Graham and Collier then sit down with the reunited group and ask, "Okay, here's what we promised you on the day you started. Where have we hit the mark, and where have we missed it?" They listen and then get to work addressing any deficiencies or inconsistencies.[11]

And that's only the beginning. Once a week, Graham and Collier each try to take an employee to lunch, just to hear what's going on. Once every month, people are chosen randomly to meet for lunch with the CEO. One of the topics up for discussion is "What do you like (not like) about the way things work around here?" Each of the company's three divisions also meets independently every month to discuss what's happening internally in their division. David and Claude join these meetings to fill them in about what's going on in the other two divisions.

> *A company cannot possibly hire enough managers and issue enough policy manuals to get all its employees to do what it wants them to do!*

At SAS Institute, the software developer outside of Raleigh, North Carolina (no relation to SAS Airlines of Sweden), Public Affairs Manager Les Hamashima apparently knows that in order for employees to understand and truly accept the mission of the company, the inculcation process will take time and lots of it. They don't try to imprint the mission of SAS onto the minds of new employees and expect them to be able to appreciate it right away. It is a process that takes much more than one day of orientation and the memorization of the mission statement. It is something that can only be built through day-to-day interaction with fellow SAS employees who are already living the mission. The values of the company—that the company exists because of the customer— become apparent by the examples other employees set.

SAS Institute Revenue

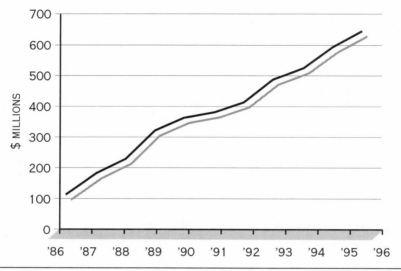

Source: SAS Institute Corporation and Financial Results, 1997.

Regardless of where people get the "word," without it a company cannot *possibly* hire enough managers and issue enough policy manuals to get all its employees to do what it wants them to do! Just ask someone like U.S. Postmaster General Marvin Runyon, who has the unenviable task of righting an organization that has tried it the other way around. Yet no matter what size the company, if the words on the mission statement do not match the reality of the work environment, employees will turn cynical and regard management's efforts as only so much corporate propaganda. Most importantly, their Commitment will not be forthcoming. Good information will determine whether the people in your organization, or any organization, are going to be truly Committed to a common purpose, or merely compliant with orders from above and just along for the ride.

HIGH EXPECTATIONS BEGET
HIGH PERFORMANCE

When it comes to Commitment, there is no middle ground. People are either passengers or they're crew. They are either Committed (yes, that's with a capital "C") or they are not. If they fall into the latter category, as much as you might want to believe otherwise, it's probably not because *they're* stupid, lazy, or mean-spirited. Certainly, a few are, but in the main, people perform the way they do because we haven't done *our* part as leaders to get them enrolled for the journey. (Remember, you get what you expect.)

To do that, we have to show them the *big picture*. According to Jack Stack, who brought Springfield Remanufacturing back from the brink, "The big picture is all about motivation. It's giving people the reason for doing the job, the purpose of working. If you're going to play a game, you have to understand what it means to win. When you show people the big picture, you define winning."[12]

In a 1994 employee opinion survey involving nearly 80,000 people from a multitude of companies, employees were asked whether or not upper management provided them ample information about the company's goals. Fairly straightforward question, right? Well, in the minds of more than 40 percent of the respondents, the answer was "no." Now, if you put any credence at all in Jack Stack's experience, that suggests that in at least 40 percent of those cases, people had no hope whatsoever of winning. Face it, if we cannot or will not give our folks straightforward information about where the ship is headed, how can we *possibly* ask them to sign on?

High expectations create an environment where both individual and company growth can occur. Each and every one of us wants desperately to be a winner. No one gets up in the morning and says to themselves, "I want to go LOSE today." However, people often don't know *how* to win in their jobs. Therefore, they either have to be shown, or else everyone loses while managers stand idly by. Too often, "winning" is defined in terms that are overly dry (does the name Bob Dole mean anything to you?);

sterile (take a look at your own company's strategic plan or "vision statements"); or completely irrelevant to the intended audience (Company X wants to achieve ROCE of 16.2 percent). **Come on, get real!!!** Dr. Martin Luther King Jr. didn't launch an entire movement with the words, "I have a strategic plan!"

CHAPTER SUMMARY

1. *Contented Cows* are *Committed Cows.*

2. Employees won't part with their "discretionary effort" for just any old reason. They must have what they consider to be good and compelling reasons. The "cause" must be impeccably clear, incredibly compelling, and it's got to square with their sensibilities.

3. Far too few employees know what the company does, where it's going, what it stands for, believes in, and where they fit in.

4. When it comes to Commitment, there's no middle ground—you either are or you aren't.

5. Committed employees are the only ones capable of delivering the kind of quality and service needed to compete.

6. Managers in the *Contented Cow* companies communicate, through word and deed, in every way imaginable, what the company is all about. The word "overcommunication" isn't even in their lexicon.

7. High expectations beget high performance.

THE PATH TO COMMITMENT

When the organization has a clear sense of its purpose, direction, and desired future state, and when this image is widely shared, individuals are able to find their own roles both in the organization and the larger society of which they are a part. They gain a sense of importance as they are transformed from robots blindly following instructions to human beings engaged in a creative and purposeful venture.

—Bennis, Warren & Nanus, Burt - *Leaders*

SO WHAT SHOULD YOU DO TO GET PEOPLE COMMITTED?

We believe there are four specific information needs to be met to achieve high levels of employee Commitment. In short, these are things your employees need, want, and have a right to know:

1. WHAT IS THIS COMPANY ALL ABOUT?

Your people need to know what the organization stands for and what it believes in. What is *really* important? What kinds of things, if they do them, will get them promoted? What'll get them fired? No, they do not want a long list of rules and regulations, or the type of pablum put out by your PR or HR department, just the plain, unadulterated facts.

NO IDENTITY CRISIS AT J&J

One organization which has demonstrated clear and consistent superiority communicating its identity is Johnson & Johnson. In a short, 308-word document known simply as "The Credo,"* they have effectively articulated just about everything anyone needs to know about what the company stands for and deems important. The Credo isn't something they cooked up just last week. It has been around about as long as their Band-Aids (since 1943 to be exact). Although it is subjected to regular internal review, scarcely a word of it has ever been changed. While many companies may have such hallowed documents stashed away in their vaults, it is doubtful that any could demonstrate as convincingly as J&J has that they actually mean it and believe what's printed on the paper.

J&J openly discusses their Credo with prospective employees, makes sure new hires get a copy of it, publishes it on the cover of their annual reports, and most importantly, they *live* it. Like in 1982, when the company successfully dealt with one of the greatest corporate crises in modern times: the Tylenol scare.

*JOHNSON & JOHNSON'S CREDO

We believe our first responsibility is to the doctors, nurses and patients, to mothers and fathers and all others who use our products and services. In meeting their needs everything we do must be of high quality. We must constantly strive to reduce our costs in order to maintain reasonable prices. Customers' orders must be serviced promptly and accurately. Our suppliers and distributors must have an opportunity to make a fair profit.

We are responsible to our employees, the men and women who work with us throughout the world. Everyone must be considered as an individual. We must respect their dignity and recognize their merit. They must have a sense of security in their jobs. Compensation must be fair and adequate, and working conditions clean, orderly and safe. We must be mindful of ways to help our employees fulfill their family responsibilities. Employees must feel free to make suggestions and complaints. There must be equal opportunity for employment, development and advancement for those qualified. We must provide competent management, and their actions must be just and ethical.

We are responsible to the communities in which we live and work and to the world community as well. We must be good citizens - support good works and charities and bear our fair share of taxes. We must encourage civic improvements and better health and education. We must maintain in good order the property we are privileged to use, protecting the environment and natural resources.

Our final responsibility is to our stockholders. Business must make a sound profit. We must experiment with new ideas. Research must be carried on, innovative programs developed and mistakes paid for. New equipment must be purchased, new facilities provided and new products launched. Reserves must be created to provide for adverse times. When we operate according to these principles, the stockholders should realize a fair return.

Source: 1996 Johnson & Johnson Annual Report

By his own admission, former J&J CEO Jim Burke spent upwards of 40 percent of his time communicating the Credo—not developing it, explaining it! While some might find it excessive for a CEO to spend that much of his or her time engaged in communicating what the organization stands for and where it's going, we would argue that it's the single most important job they've got!

According to Burke, "All of our management is geared to profit on a day-to-day basis. That's part of the business of being in business. But too often, in this and other businesses, people are inclined to think, 'We'd better do this because if we don't, it's going to show up on the figures over the short-term.' This document allows them to say, 'Wait a minute. I don't have to do that.' The management has told me that they're interested in operating under this set of principles, so I won't."[1]

Some might think it a little odd that only in the fourth (and final) paragraph does J&J's Credo refer to the company's obligations to its stockholders. The first three paragraphs deal with topics like customers, employees, and the communities of which they are a part. But before you start feeling too sorry for their stockholders, take a look at *Fortune's* 1996 "Most Admired List" (J&J ranks fourth); *Business Week's* 1996 list of "Most Valuable

Companies" (J&J ranks eighth); and the fact that between 1985 and 1995, J&J earned an eye-popping average annual return to investors of 23.1 percent.

IN THE HAY AT KINGSTON

While communicating the what-we're-all-about message can be as simple as telling employees clearly and showing them *consistently*, remember, they'll be watching your bellybutton. The corporate bellybutton is precisely what the 527 employees of Kingston Technologies in Fountain Valley, California—the world's largest manufacturer of computer memory and enhancement products—were watching when Kingston founders David Sun and John Tu sold the company in August, 1996 to Softbank Corp. of Japan. The employees were not relegated to the status of observers for long, however, as Sun and Tu forked over $40 million in bonuses to them. The bonuses resulted in an average distribution of more than $75,000 per employee, with some people earning as much as $300,000![2]

Upon hearing Kingston's story, everyone's first reaction is, "I'd be committed too, for those bucks!" But the point, argue the founders, is that the bonuses were the *effect* of the high commitment, not its cause, which is perfectly consistent with the company's espoused beliefs: "Kingston's culture is 'employees are number one,'" says Sun. "If we can bring the employees together, then you win the customer everywhere."[3]

To be sure, Sun and Tu had no more obligation to share the wealth than their employees did to part with copious amounts of their own discretionary effort in the first place. Yet part with it they did, like the Kingston technician who flew from sunny California to snowy New York for the weekend to repair a system problem. Okay, that much was his job. But when the problem turned out to be a minor, 15-minute fix, rather than taking off for the rest of the weekend, the technician decided to stay and help the customer with some other computer glitches he was experiencing. "My return ticket wasn't 'til Sunday night anyway," he reasoned, knowing his conscientious actions "above and beyond" duty's call had made the company a Kingston customer for life.

Conscientious employees at Kingston seem to be the rule rather than the exception. Take the service call which came into Kingston's Fountain Valley office from a Southern California hotel customer one evening about 6:30. The caller explained that the hotel was in a real pickle, but they couldn't afford to bring the whole system down until after two the next morning. They had to keep the reservations system available, or lose tons of money. The Kingston employee, a fairly new recruit, took it upon himself to go home for a few hours and get some sleep. Then he got up at 1:00 A.M. and drove to the hotel, where he stayed up all night and fixed the problem at a time when it was convenient for the customer. To top it off, he showed up on time for work the next morning and worked his full schedule. Did he have to do that? Of course not, no more than Sun and Tu had to pay out the big bonuses. See? What goes around really does come around.

"Sellin' Chicken"

The mission at Chick-fil-A is about as clear and uncomplicated as it gets. While I was conducting a Coaching Skills workshop at the company's headquarters near the Atlanta airport, one class-member volunteered that "[Founder and CEO] Truett Cathy has always been very clear about what we do here at Chick-fil-A: *We sell chicken*. It's as simple as that. And no matter what you're doing, if it pertains to *sellin' chicken*, then you're probably doing the right thing. If whatever you're doing gets in the way of *sellin' chicken*, or if it doesn't have anything to do with *sellin' chicken*, you better not let Truett find out about it. And he finds out about everything."

Truett Cathy never saw any reason to micro-manage. For nearly 50 years he had been very clear. In simple, easy-to-understand terms, he told people that as long as their activities promoted *sellin' chicken*—within the parameters of the company's unusually high standard of ethics—it was sanctioned, condoned, and encouraged. That answered a lot of questions, and eliminated the need for a lot of hefty "Sears-like" policy manuals.

At one point in the workshop, I accompanied a small group from the class to a breakout room on another floor. As the elevator door opened, there stood Truett, on his way up to his office from the basement. After warm greetings to each of the seminar participants by name and an introduction to me, whom he didn't know from Adam's house cat, he asked interestedly, "Whatchall doin'?" They all chimed in chorus, *"Sellin' chicken!"* Truett beamed, and he probed no further.

2. WHERE ARE WE GOING AND WHY?

People want to know what journey you are asking them to sign up for. Do you plan to go to the moon by the end of the decade? The White House in 2001? Ten billion dollars in revenue by the year 2000? The Super Bowl in five years? Or what? Sadly, most organizations fail and fail miserably on this one. They either have no credible sense of mission, or they can't articulate it. Either way, it spells disaster.

If people don't know full well where your ship is headed, they can't possibly help you get there. Talking about this very task at GE, Jack Welch said that the company must "define its destiny in broad but clear terms. You need an overarching message, something big, but simple and understandable."[4] Howard Putnam (former Southwest Airlines president and CEO) explained the very practical implications of the problem: "Most companies fail in their growth because they don't have a vision. They don't know where to go. When you have a vision and someone comes to you with some convoluted idea, you can hold it up to the vision and ask "Does it fit? Does it fly? If not, don't bother me." A vision must be so strong that it can outweigh the egos of managers that might want to take off in a different direction."[5]

Where there is no vision, the people perish.

—Franklin D. Roosevelt

LOST IN SPACE

Over its course in history of being both a winning and later a losing organization, NASA has exemplified the importance of the sense of mission perhaps better than anyone. Following President Kennedy's declaration that the nation would put a man on the moon and return him safely to Earth by the end of the decade, the thousands of men and women who make up NASA proceeded to do the very best work of their professional lives in order to make that dream a reality.

Once the "moonshot" had been accomplished, however, no goal as compelling was put in its place, and the agency lost sight of where it was going. Tragically, as evidenced by the space shuttle *Challenger* disaster, we all know where it went.

GUARANTEEING A WIN

One of the hands-down winners in the world of sports has got to be Jimmy Johnson, the former head coach of the Dallas Cowboys who currently holds the same position with the Miami Dolphins. When he took over an ailing Cowboys team in 1989, Johnson proclaimed that in five years the team would be going to the Superbowl. How's that for mission clarity? Johnson didn't say they would be going to the playoffs, win the division, or settle for a winning record. Nothing less than the Superbowl would do. Although Johnson misspoke (it only took four years), the lesson for us is that because the mission was Bold, Clear, and Meaningful, it was also compelling. It captured the hearts and minds not just of a football franchise, but an entire city.

Speaking about his bold public statements prior to the 1990, 1991, and 1992 seasons, Johnson said, "All three times the media looked at me like 'this guy's nuts.' But all three times, our players got a message that was strong and positive about high expectations, and all three times they lived up to the expectations."[6] The importance of the part about high expectations cannot be overstated. People who show up for work at your place or ours have a need for some very basic— and affordable—things, and one of them is the opportunity to do meaningful and significant work. Modest expectations inspire modest work!

THE CRAYON TEST

In his book, *Beating the Street*, former Fidelity Magellan Fund manager Peter Lynch makes the case that investors ought not put their money into anything which "cannot be explained with a crayon."[7] Given the complexity of today's financial markets, that's probably good advice. It is every bit as useful, however, for those of us who are entrusted with explaining to others where our organization is headed. If you can't convey that message, graphically and credibly, with the very same crayon (literally), then you can't explain it, and your people ought not (and probably won't) invest in it!

Once the journey and its purpose have been made impeccably clear, however, it's time for everyone (no exceptions) to either enthusiastically get in the boat and start rowing, or be thrown overboard. As the late David Packard (Hewlett's partner) pointed out, "There can be no place for half-hearted interest or effort. ... A high degree of enthusiasm should be encouraged at all levels; in particular, the people in high management positions must not only be enthusiastic themselves, but they must be able to engender enthusiasm among their associates."[8] Failure to adhere to this "iron law" will wreak havoc within and inevitably doom any organization.

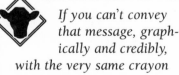

If you can't convey that message, graphically and credibly, with the very same crayon (literally), then you can't explain it, and your people ought not (and probably won't) invest in it!

3. How Do We Plan to Get There?

We believe that the *process* an organization uses to determine its destination is far less important than the methods used to communicate it and the level of discipline employed to get and keep people moving in the same direction. After the destination becomes clear, people have a right to know how you intend to get there. What's the game plan for achieving your destination? It's not that the entire plan needs to be laid out (in fact you are probably better off if there's a little room for improvisation), but the first two or three steps would be a great start.

PLAYSCRIPTING

The wisdom of this approach was made apparent by former San Francisco 49ers head coach Bill Walsh. Over the course of his illustrious career, Walsh developed a practice he called "play scripting." On the day before a game, Walsh would simply make a list of the first 10 or 12 offensive plays his team would run the next day, and then share that list with his players in their Saturday night meeting. The result? According to Walsh, "The players liked it. They felt it eliminated some pregame anxiety, because they knew ahead of time what they would be doing on the first series. They had a chance to think about it, and most of them said they even slept better."[9] In 10 seasons under Walsh, the 49ers won three Superbowls and six NFL Western Division titles. Playscripting is now an indispensable part of game preparation for offensive coordinators throughout the NFL.

4. How do I fit in?

Finally, people need to know what role you want them to play, and what it is you'll be expecting of them. Earlier we made the point that you've got to get the *big picture* indelibly burned into your employees' gray matter. You do. But people don't work day-to-day in the big picture. Instead, the proof is in the details, which, individually and taken together, send powerful messages that either confirm and lend support to, or contradict the big picture.

As organizations get larger, it's inevitable that people will begin to lose sight of where they fit in and how their contributions matter. Without regular and vigorous reinforcement on this point, people ultimately conclude that their contributions really do not matter all that much, and the decline in their effort is at hand. People who have come to believe that their role isn't all that important stand idly by and watch poor quality stuff go down the line; or a disgruntled customer go out the door; and they definitely don't hustle. Remember what Jim Barksdale said? "Motivated people move faster."

> As organizations get larger, it's virtually inevitable that people will begin to lose sight of where they fit in and how their contributions matter.

We *all* want to be a part of something important, and we want to play a meaningful role. Imagine for a moment how difficult it would be for *you* to remain Committed to something if you were the least bit uncertain about whether or not your efforts really mattered. We're often reminded of this point whenever there's a snowstorm of any size in our nation's capital, and the airwaves are immediately filled with announcements for government employees that "only people in essential positions need report for work." Now, deep down, who the hell wants something they spend eight hours a day doing to be deemed nonessential?

The moment your people feel that it's no longer important for them to do their very best work, your company has started down a very steep and slippery slope. Sorry for the replay, but the point bears repeating: "High expectations breed high performance."

An individual without information cannot take responsibility. An individual who is given information cannot help but take responsibility.[10]
—Jan Carlzon

CHAPTER SUMMARY

1. Commitment starts with the *big picture*
   - What is this company all about?
   - Where are we going, and why?
   - How do we plan to get there?
   - How do I fit in?

2. You've got to be able to articulate it simply and credibly. Remember the crayons!

SECTION THREE

CONTENTED COWS ARE CARED ABOUT

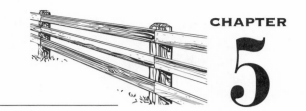

FIRST YOU FEED
THE TROOPS

The best and most successful commanders ... are those who win the respect, confidence, and affection of their subordinates by justice and firmness, tempered by kindness.

—General John Schofield

It was a bleak and windy night on the remote island of Orkney—off the northern coast of Scotland—during World War II. Sergeant Major Jim Prentice of the Gordon Highlanders, a Scottish regiment of the British Army, was leading his men on maneuvers in preparation for the battles in Burma soon to come. Darkness had descended before four o'clock that afternoon, and now snow was falling at ten. The men were too far from their camp to get back without danger of freezing, so they were more than relieved to see the dim lights of a farm oasis not far ahead. They hoped the inhabitants would extend the hospitality of their barn for the war effort.

Sergeant Major Prentice knocked on the door of the farmhouse and awakened the farmer from his warm bed on that cold night. When he asked only if his men could sleep in the barn, the man patriotically gave his consent, but on the stipulation that all 30 of them first have a hot meal in his kitchen. The farmer roused his wife and kids from their sleep and the family prepared an inelegant feast of ground beef, potatoes, turnips, carrots, and pancakes. Six at a time, the soldiers warmed themselves and filled their insides in the farmer's tiny kitchen, while the others waited appreciatively in the barn.

The farmer's 9-year-old son watched curiously as Prentice, obviously the ranking soldier among them, ushered each group into the house. Only when all the troops had been served did he take a place at the table and eat. Curious at this unexpected behavior, the boy, who had been invited by the sergeant major to join him at the rough-hewn table, asked, "Why'd you go last? You're the leader!"

Prentice looked the young man in the eye and said with both conviction and instruction, "First you feed the troops. They're no good to you hungry."

More than 40 years went by before Prentice returned to that island at the edge of his own country. This time he came not as a soldier, but as a tourist, with his wife and grown daughter at his side. While his family toured the remains of a 5,000-year-old burial mound, he took a walk—a "wee donner" as he called it— up the road, as was his custom.

Prentice had not gone more than a few yards before he stumbled onto ground that bore a strange air of familiarity. As he wandered up to the house in the middle of the vast property, a man in his early fifties approached him. "Is there something I can help you with, sir?" Prentice explained the aura he sensed and began to ask the man questions about the farm. Then because the man seemed interested, he related to him the story of that night in 1940 when the kind farmer had taken in his troops and not only let them sleep in the barn, but ... "First you feed the troops!" the man interrupted, shaking a knowing finger at the wizened face he now recognized.

"You're not the wee boy!" exclaimed Prentice.

"None other," said the farmer, and then he proceeded to bring his old friend up to date on the farm which he had inherited from his parents. His business had grown nearly fourfold in four decades! Until this conversation, Prentice had given no thought to the influence his simple act and single remark might have had on the young boy. Yet less than 10 years after the soldiers stopped by on that snowy evening, he had begun to take over the daily management of the farm. "I've always remembered what that sergeant major told me at the table," the farmer reminisced, "and even when the harvest was slim, and it was mighty slim some years, I've always made sure the hands working the farm had what they needed. You know, they're no good to you hungry."

HUNGRY TROOPS: A COMPARATIVE STUDY IN WAR AND PEACE

In its 1991 coverage of the first and only four days of the ground phase of the Gulf War, CNN showed countless clips of bedraggled Iraqi soldiers emerging—hands high in the air—from their desert encampments and surrendering to U.S.-led coalition forces. What CNN did not show were the commanding officers of those troops. Not because CNN goofed, but because the officers, the so-called leaders of those troops, were not to be found. They were gone! Rather than stick it out with their men and risk an almost certain fate, they had vanished into the night.

Closer to home, but in roughly the same time frame, Texas businessman Ross Perot was leveling one blistering attack after another on the management of a major U.S. corporation. The corporation was General Motors, about which one can presume Perot knew more than most. On the heels of yet another "bad year," GM had served up huge bonus payouts to top managers, while at the same time failing to contribute the first nickel to the company's profit sharing plans. Hardly one to be anti-business or anti-bonus, Perot's point was simply that, "First you feed the troops. ..." Where have we heard that before?

While it would be both foolish and terribly unjust to paint the officers of GM and the Iraqi military with the same brush, they nonetheless were guilty of some of the same mistakes, and the larger organizations of which they were a part suffered as a result. In short, neither cared. In the case of GM, they didn't care about their people, who, in turn, cared less about the products they were making and the droves of customers who had stopped buying those products because they weren't very good.

CARING CAN'T BE FAKED

First, let's establish the fact that caring is not a program, a technique, or something that can be taught or bought. It's not a *quid pro quo*. Caring is not about coddling people, making them feel comfortable, or providing false hope or security.

Your employees are a lot more rational than they are given credit for. They really don't expect a "free ride." They know, for example that you can't insulate them from anxiety and job stress any more than their homeowner's policy can keep a hurricane from roaring through their neighborhood. They also know that you really can't always guarantee the security of their jobs. Yet they still expect you to be fiercely Committed to things like being scrupulously honest with them, believing in them, helping them succeed, and being there for them when they need it. Rightly so. They know that when push comes to shove, you either care or you don't, and that nobody is a good enough actor or actress to fake it for long.

According to Tommy Lasorda, former manager of the Los Angeles Dodgers, the wise manager goes out of his or her way on a regular basis to let people know how important they are. "I want my players to know that I appreciate what they do for me. I want them to know that I depend on them. When you, as a leader of people, are naive enough to think that you, not your players, won the game, then you're in bad shape."[1] No doubt, that's one of the reasons Lasorda was frequently the first one out of the dugout to congratulate his players for making a big play.

As former America West CEO Mike Conway put it, "It's not that complicated. First you've got to care, and then you've got to demonstrate that you care by your actions because there is a natural skepticism out there. It's just not that complicated, but you've got to be committed to caring."[2]

AMERICA WEST AIRLINES

	1995	1996
NUMBER OF AIRCRAFT	93	101
AVAILABLE SEAT MILES (000)	19,421,451	21,624,529
REVENUE PASSENGER MILES (000)	13,312,742	15,321,422
PASSENGER ENPLANEMENTS	13,504	14,699

Source: America West PR Newswire, 1997.

In July of 1996, we met Angela Perry, a seven-year Delta flight attendant, who echoed the exact same sentiment but from an employee's perspective: "It all comes down to whether or not we believe that our management cares. If they do, we'll bend over backwards to look out for the company and our customers. If not, well ..."3

> *I feel that you have to be with your employees through all their difficulties, that you have to be interested in them personally. I want them to know that Southwest will always be there for them.*
> —Herb Kelleher, Southwest Airlines CEO

Caring is not a "photo-op." Rather, it's an attitude that's reflected by personal and organizational priorities. Organizations that care about their people take pains to ensure that human considerations are in the forefront of their decision making process when they develop corporate programs and policies, for example; or while acquiring and designing facilities, equipment, and systems; or when scheduling and arranging work. This is not something they do some of the time, or most of the time, but *always*, even when it's unpopular or seemingly less profitable to do so.

Without a doubt, there are degrees of caring and associated degrees of personal sacrifice which reflect how much you care. Despite what you may think of his political escapades, Ross Perot, founder and former chairman of Electronic Data Systems (which he later sold to General Motors) has provided one of the most visible and courageous examples in recent times of a leader who cares about his troops. As chronicled in Ken Follett's book, *On Wings of Eagles*, in 1979, Perot insisted on participating personally in the daring and dangerous rescue of two EDS employees who were being held hostage in Iran. According to Perot, "I talked Paul [Chiapparone] and Bill [Gaylord] into going over there [Iran], and I'm going to get them out."4 He did, and in the process demonstrated one of the most basic tenets of caring:

You've got to let people know you care about them by your physical presence when they are dealing with adversity.

> *Sincerity is the most important part of positive treatment. The only thing worse than a coach or CEO who doesn't care about his people is one who pretends to care. People can spot a phony every time. They know he doesn't care about them, and worse, his act insults their intelligence.*
>
> —Jimmy Johnson

THE CUSTOMER COMES SECOND

Rosenbluth Travel CEO Hal Rosenbluth has done what some might consider going way out on a limb by titling his book *The Customer Comes Second*. He means *after* his employees. Southwest's Herb Kelleher says the same goes for his organization. Reportedly, he has invited more than one Southwest customer to find another airline when they became a bit too pushy or abusive with his people. These examples are not meant to suggest that "caring" organizations are at all cavalier about making money. On the contrary, they just happen to believe that doing right by their people will inevitably find its way to the bottom line—a much healthier bottom line, in fact. As evidenced by the following chart, which reflects the number of complaints filed per 100,000 passengers, Southwest customers apparently aren't too put out with them. (see Figure 5.1)

An organization's degree of caring is evidenced not by what it says but by what it does. (After all, what company in its right right mind would claim not to care?)

Since its inception, FedEx has espoused a rather simple business philosophy known as P–S–P (for People-Service-Profit). The fact that the "People" part comes first is no accident. The company attempts to demonstrate their philosophy in a host of ways, personnel decisions being one of them. As one might expect in such a high performance organization, performance standards

FIGURE 5.1

COMPLAINTS PER 100,000 PASSENGERS (JAN. - SEPT. '96)

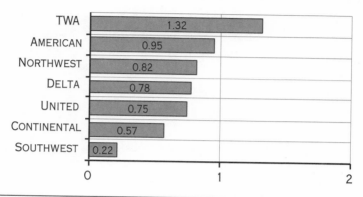

Source: U.S. Dept. of Transportation

and expectations are quite high, and not everyone measures up. But the quickest ticket out of that organization goes not to someone who has blown their budget or even disappointed a customer, but to anyone—especially a manager—who is disrespectful of or abusive toward another human being.

Let's go back to lunch at Renee's Sandwich Store. One of the reasons we think she has kept the same folks making her "Incredible Roast Beef Creations" and frying frozen potatoes for so long is that she cares about those often nameless faces who feed the masses each day. "These are the people who are making me money!" she shrieks as though it should be obvious, and she's right. Renee lends her employees money when they are in a pinch (which isn't often), and not one has ever abused her kindness. They all have their evenings free, so at least three times a year she takes the crew out to dinner. She gives them paid vacation—in a sandwich shop! And during the Christmas season, she puts up a little tree—like a special holiday tip jar—to which many appreciative customers paper clip "gifts." Who says money can't grow on trees?

"I care about them, and they care about me, and about each other. It's great," says this strong businesswoman with a personality that doesn't suffer slackers lightly. She once offered an employee the extra bedroom in her house, rent-free. Why? Because she had a social obligation to take in the down-and-out? No, Renee explains that "she was a damn good worker, and I knew that if she had a place to stay that was nearby, she'd be at work everyday. I was right, and she made us both a bunch of money."

> *A leader should possess human understanding and consideration for others. Men are not robots and should not be treated as such. I do not by any means suggest coddling. But men are intelligent, complicated beings who will respond favorably to human understanding and consideration. By these means their leader will get maximum effort from each of them. He will also get loyalty.*
>
> —General Omar Bradley

GM: WHAT WENT WRONG?

Let's take time out right now to debunk a fairly popular myth. Caring about your people does not equate to lavishing them with money and expensive benefits, increases and extras which they haven't earned, the market doesn't require, and you can't afford. General Motors has been guilty of all three in its frequent capitulations to the United Auto Workers. Absent good and compelling reasons for these actions, GM has done itself and its employees (not to mention customers and shareholders) a huge disservice. Everyone involved knows it, too. Not unlike a "one night stand"; it may have felt good at the time, but they've been paying for it ever since.

One need only look at what has happened to GM's share of the U.S. car market and to their market value to know that something went seriously wrong. Between 1978 and 1995, for example, their share of the U.S. car and truck market slid from 46 to 32 percent.[5]

FIGURE 5.2

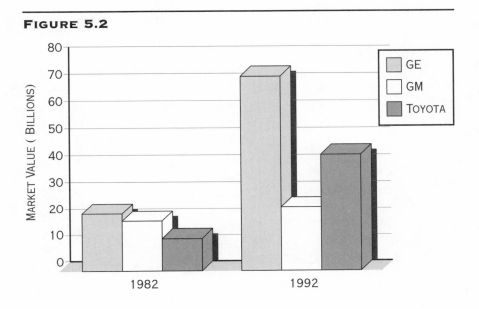

During the '80s and early '90s, when other industrial giants such as General Electric and Toyota saw their market value leap in excess of 20 percent annually, GM's managed barely a 5 percent annual gain.[6] (see Figure 5.2)

> *People don't care how much you know until they know how much you care.*
> —Anonymous

By providing benefits such as fully funded, zero-deductible health, vision, and dental care; supplemental unemployment insurance; and the like, by early 1996, GM had ratcheted its production labor costs into the $40-per-hour vicinity. This unfortunate development gave competitors such as parts maker Bosch an immediate cost advantage of roughly $20 per hour. Now, you've got to be pretty damned good to give your competitors a $20-an-hour head start and still expect to beat them in the marketplace. It would seem that when the cost of benefits started exceeding the cost of the steel needed to make cars, someone might have deduced that something was terribly amiss.

Instead, faced with losing roughly one-third of their U.S. car market share, continuing quality problems, an ocean of red ink ($23.5 billion in 1992 alone), and the loss of a sizable hunk of their stockholders' equity,[7] GM behaved just like the slow-boiled laboratory frog—the only difference being that the hand controlling the burner was their own! Asked by *Fortune* to explain what went wrong, then-GM boss Roger Smith was quoted as saying, "I don't know. It's a mysterious thing."[8]

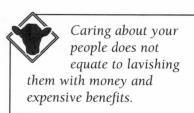

Caring about your people does not equate to lavishing them with money and expensive benefits.

Though admittedly a matter of opinion, we happen to believe that the problems at GM had far more to do with the attitudes and commitment level of its workforce (demoralized by an inattentive and uncaring management and a fractious relationship with the UAW) than with engineering, design, marketing, finance, or manufacturing processes. Think about it: GM enjoyed a huge brand name advantage; employed some of the best designers and marketing minds on the planet; had spent enough of their capital reserves on technological improvement to have bought Toyota outright; and yet they were still making crummy cars! Go figure.

Commenting on the company's partial recovery since the dark days of the late '80s and early '90s, Vice Chairman Harry B. Pearce said, "It is more than morale; it is a real feeling that people can make a difference. As big as this company is, you can always worry about people feeling they can have any impact. ..."[9] Indeed, Pearce's cause for concern had been effectively confirmed a couple of years earlier by Mark McKinney, one of his own production workers, who said, "To General Motors, you're a number. You're number 7795. This department needs a body, that department needs a body. ..."[10] People who feel they are nothing but a number or a body simply will not part with much of their discretionary effort.